**TEACHER'S PET PUBLICATIONS**

LITPLAN TEACHER PACK
for
The Witch of Blackbird Pond
based on the book by
Elizabeth George Speare

Written by
Mary B. Collins

© 1996 Teacher's Pet Publications
All Rights Reserved

This **LitPlan** for Elizabeth George Speare's
The Witch of Blackbird Pond
has been brought to you by Teacher's Pet Publications, Inc.

Copyright Teacher's Pet Publications 1996
11504 Hammock Point
Berlin MD 21811

Only the student materials in this unit plan (such as worksheets,
study questions, and tests) may be reproduced multiple times
for use in the purchaser's classroom.

For any additional copyright questions,
contact Teacher's Pet Publications.

www.tpet.com

TABLE OF CONTENTS - *The Witch of Blackbird Pond*

Introduction	5
Unit Objectives	7
Reading Assignment Sheet	8
Unit Outline	9
Study Questions (Short Answer)	13
Quiz/Study Questions (Multiple Choice)	23
Pre-reading Vocabulary Worksheets	41
Lesson One (Introductory Lesson)	59
Nonfiction Assignment Sheet	61
Oral Reading Evaluation Form	
Writing Assignment 1	69
Writing Assignment 2	75
Writing Assignment 3	76
Writing Evaluation Form	77
Vocabulary Review Activities	73
Extra Writing Assignments/Discussion ?s	71
Unit Review Activities	79
Unit Tests	83
Unit Resource Materials	119
Vocabulary Resource Materials	135

A FEW NOTES ABOUT THE AUTHOR
Elizabeth George Speare

Speare, Elizabeth George (1908-1994) U. S. author of historical fiction for children, born on Nov. 21, 1908 in Melrose, Mass. Each of Speare's books was meticulously researched so that historical details were appropriate for the period. Her characters were also well rounded, and she appealed to her readers by drawing them into history with ease.

Speare studied at Smith College and graduated from Boston University with a B.A. degree in 1930 and an M.A. in 1932. She later taught English in high schools in Massachusetts. She was awarded the Newbery Medal in 1959 for 'The Witch of Blackbird Pond' (1958) and in 1962 for 'The Bronze Bow' (1961). She also wrote 'Calico Captive' (1957) and 'Life in Colonial America' (1963), as well as a novel for adults, 'The Prospering' (1967). Her last children's novel, 'Sign of the Beaver' (1983), won a Newbery Medal and the Scott O'Dell award for historical fiction. Speare died on November 15, 1994.

INTRODUCTION - *Witch of Blackbird Pond*

This unit has been designed to develop students' reading, writing, thinking, and language skills through exercises and activities related to *The Witch of Blackbird Pond* by Elizabeth George Speare. It includes seventeen lessons, supported by extra resource materials.

The **introductory lesson** introduces students to the theme of moving to a place far away. Following the introductory activity, students are given a transition to explain how the activity relates to the book they are about to read. Following the transition, students are given the materials they will be using during the unit. At the end of the lesson, students begin the pre-reading work for the first reading assignment.

The **reading assignments** are approximately thirty pages each; some are a little shorter while others are a little longer. Students have approximately 15 minutes of pre-reading work to do prior to each reading assignment. This pre-reading work involves reviewing the study questions for the assignment and doing some vocabulary work for 8 to 10 vocabulary words they will encounter in their reading.

The **study guide questions** are fact-based questions; students can find the answers to these questions right in the text. These questions come in two formats: short answer or multiple choice. The best use of these materials is probably to use the short answer version of the questions as study guides for students (since answers will be more complete), and to use the multiple choice version for occasional quizzes. It might be a good idea to make transparencies of your answer keys for the overhead projector.

The **vocabulary work** is intended to enrich students' vocabularies as well as to aid in the students' understanding of the book. Prior to each reading assignment, students will complete a two-part worksheet for approximately 8 to 10 vocabulary words in the upcoming reading assignment. Part I focuses on students' use of general knowledge and contextual clues by giving the sentence in which the word appears in the text. Students are then to write down what they think the words mean based on the words' usage. Part II nails down the definitions of the words by giving students dictionary definitions of the words and having students match the words to the correct definitions based on the words' contextual usage. Students should then have an understanding of the words when they meet them in the text.

After each reading assignment, students will go back and formulate answers for the study guide questions. Discussion of these questions serves as a **review** of the most important events and ideas presented in the reading assignments.

After students complete reading the work, there is a lesson devoted to the **extra discussion questions/writing assignments**. These questions focus on interpretation, critical analysis and personal response, employing a variety of thinking skills and adding to the students' understanding of the novel.

Following the discussion questions, there is a **vocabulary review** lesson which pulls together all of the fragmented vocabulary lists for the reading assignments and gives students a review of all of the words they have studied.

The **group activity** has students working in small groups to research and discuss several nonfiction topics related to the ideas in the story. The group activity is followed by a **reports and discussion** session in which the groups share their research about the topics with the entire class; thus, the entire class is exposed to information about many different ideas related to the story.

There are three **writing assignments** in this unit, each with the purpose of informing, persuading, or having students express personal opinions. The first assignment is to inform: students explain the information they found in their research. The second assignment is to express personal opinions/feelings: students write a composition in which they complete the sentence, "Ah, if I could sail away...." The third assignment is to practice persuasive writing: students create a travel brochure for the place to which they sailed away in the second writing assignment.

The **nonfiction reading assignment** is combined with the group activity in this unit. Students are required to read a piece of nonfiction related in some way to *The Witch of Blackbird Pond*, specifically relating to the topics they have been assigned. After reading their nonfiction pieces, students will fill out a worksheet on which they answer questions regarding facts, interpretation, criticism, and personal opinions.

The **review lesson** pulls together all of the aspects of the unit. The teacher is given four or five choices of activities or games to use which all serve the same basic function of reviewing all of the information presented in the unit.

The **unit test** comes in two formats: multiple choice or short answer. As a convenience, two different tests for each format have been included.

There are additional **support materials** included with this unit. The **Unit Resource** section includes suggestions for an in-class library, crossword and word search puzzles related to the novel, and extra vocabulary worksheets. There is a list of **bulletin board ideas** which gives the teacher suggestions for bulletin boards to go along with this unit. In addition, there is a list of **extra class activities** the teacher could choose from to enhance the unit or as a substitution for an exercise the teacher might feel is inappropriate for his/her class. **Answer keys** are located directly after the **reproducible student materials** throughout the unit. The student materials may be reproduced for use in the teacher's classroom without infringement of copyrights. No other portion of this unit may be reproduced without the written consent of Teacher's Pet Publications, Inc.

UNIT OBJECTIVES - *The Witch of Blackbird Pond*

1. Through reading *The Witch of Blackbird Pond*, students will gain a better understanding of the Puritans.

2. Students will see that moving from one area to another and becoming adjusted in one's new home has never been easy.

3. Students will learn that conflicts between individual citizens and institutions (like church and government) are a part of any historical era, not just modern times.

4. Students will demonstrate their understanding of the text on four levels: factual, interpretive, critical and personal.

5. Students will learn about the historical background for *The Witch of Blackbird Pond*.

6. Students will be given the opportunity to practice reading aloud and silently to improve their skills in each area.

7. Students will answer questions to demonstrate their knowledge and understanding of the main events and characters in *The Witch of Blackbird Pond* as they relate to the author's theme development.

8. Students will enrich their vocabularies and improve their understanding of the novel through the vocabulary lessons prepared for use in conjunction with the novel.

9. The writing assignments in this unit are geared to several purposes:
    a. To have students demonstrate their abilities to inform, to persuade, or to express their own personal ideas
        Note: Students will demonstrate ability to write effectively to <u>inform</u> by developing and organizing facts to convey information. Students will demonstrate the ability to write effectively to <u>persuade</u> by selecting and organizing relevant information, establishing an argumentative purpose, and by designing an appropriate strategy for an identified audience. Students will demonstrate the ability to write effectively to <u>express personal ideas</u> by selecting a form and its appropriate elements.
    b. To check the students' reading comprehension
    c. To make students think about the ideas presented by the novel
    d. To encourage logical thinking
    e. To provide an opportunity to practice good grammar and improve students' use of the English language.

10. Students will read aloud, report, and participate in large and small group discussions to improve their public speaking and personal interaction skills.

READING ASSIGNMENT SHEET - *The Witch of Blackbird Pond*

Date Assigned	Chapters Assigned	Completion Date
	1-3	
	4-7	
	8-10	
	11-13	
	14-16	
	17-18	
	19-21	

UNIT OUTLINE - *The Witch of Blackbird Pond*

1 Introduction PV 1-3	2 Read 1-3	3 Study ?s 1-3 PVR 4-7	4 Study ?s 4-7 PVR 8-10 Group Activity	5 Library
6 Study ?s 8-10 PVR 11-13 Group Work	7 Study ?s 11-13 PVR 14-16	8 Study ?s 14-16 Writing Assignment 1 PVR 17-18	9 Study ?s 17-18 Group Reports PVR 19-21	10 Study ?s 19-21 Group Reports
11 Extra Questions	12 Vocabulary	13 Writing Assignment 2	14 Group Writing Assignment	15 Group Writing Assignment
16 Review	17 Test			

Key: P = Preview Study Questions   V = Prereading Vocabulary Work   R = Read

STUDY GUIDE QUESTIONS

SHORT ANSWER STUDY GUIDE QUESTIONS - *The Witch of Blackbird Pond*

Chapters 1-3
1. Where did Kit live before going on this journey?
2. Where did Mistress Eaton spend her summers?
3. What was a new sensation for Kit?
4. Why did Kit jump off of the long boat?
5. Identify Goodwife Cruff.
6. How did people on the boat react when Kit said that she could swim?
7. Identify John Holbrook.
8. Why did Goodwife Cruff think Kit was a witch?
9. Identify Prudence.
10. Why did Kit live with her grandfather in Barbados?
11. Why was John surprised that Kit read plays?
12. Why weren't Kit's relatives at the dock to meet her?
13. What was Kit's feeling about Wethersfield?
14. Why was Kit's grandfather no longer wealthy?
15. Describe Matthew Wood.

Chapters 4-7
1. What kind of a woman is Rachel?
2. What was wrong with Mercy?
3. How did Matthew Wood react to Kit's giving clothes to his daughters?
4. Why did Kit have to come to Connecticut?
5. What did Judith think of Kit?
6. What are Sabbath houses?
7. What did Kit think of the church services?
8. Why did Dr. Bulkeley think Matthew was a traitor?
9. Identify William Ashby.
10. Was Judith upset about the loss of William?
11. Describe William's "call" on Kit.
12. Why was the fact that William had started building his house significant?

Chapters 8-10
1. Describe Kit's feelings about the meadows.
2. Identify Hannah Tupper.
3. What job was Kit offered?
4. What had happened to Mercy's brothers?
5. Why did Matthew Wood change after the death of his second son?

Witch of Blackbird Pond Short Answer Study Questions Page 2

6. What did Kit do to anger the schoolmasters?
7. Where did Kit go after she had been dismissed as a teacher?
8. Why did Kit go to see Mr. Kimberly?
9. Who was Hannah's seafaring friend?

Chapters 11-13
1. Who left Kit flowers?
2. Why didn't Prudence go to school?
3. How did Kit teach Prudence to read?
4. What secret did Kit discover about Mercy?
5. What did Nat and Kit do for Hannah?
6. To what did Nat compare Kit?
7. What did Matthew Wood do when he discovered that Kit had been seeing and helping Hannah Tupper?
8. Which Wood girl did John Holbrook like?
9. What did Judith think John was going to say?
10. What was Kit's response to William's marriage proposal?

Chapters 14-16
1. Where did Kit see Nat?
2. How did Kit feel about Governor Andros?
3. Why was the charter safe?
4. What happened to William's new home?
5. Who was one of the men who took part in the illumination of William's home?
6. What was Nat's punishment?
7. What did Kit teach Prudence to do (other than to read)?
8. Where did John go?

Chapters 17-18
1. What happened to Judith?
2. How did Mercy react to becoming sick?
3. What was Dr. Bulkeley's cure for the fever?
4. Where did Kit hide Hannah?
5. Why did the people want Hannah?
6. What made Kit feel guilty?
7. How did the townspeople suppose Hannah had escaped?
8. What happened to Kit?

Witch of Blackbird Pond Short Answer Study Questions Page 3

<u>Chapters 19-21</u>
1. What evidence did Goodman Cruff bring forth at the hearing?
2. How was Kit proved to be innocent?
3. What change came over Goodman Cruff when he found out that Prudence could read and write?
4. What did John do when he got home?
5. Why had William stayed away during Kit's arrest and hearing?
6. Who was going to be married?
7. How was Kit going to afford passage back to Barbados?
8. Who did Kit realize she loved?
9. What did Nat buy?

KEY: SHORT ANSWER STUDY GUIDE QUESTIONS - *The Witch of Blackbird Pond*

Chapters 1-3

1. Where did Kit live before going on this journey?
    She lived in Barbados.

2. Where did Mistress Eaton spend her summers?
    She spent summers at home in Saybrook, tending her garden.

3. What was a new sensation for Kit?
    Embarrassment was new to Kit.

4. Why did Kit jump off of the long boat?
    A little girl had lost her doll in the water, and the captain wouldn't turn around to go get it.

5. Identify Goodwife Cruff.
    She was the somber mother of the little girl who lost the doll. She clearly does not approve of Kit, and Kit clearly doesn't approve of her.

6. How did people on the boat react when Kit said that she could swim?
    They were surprised and suspicious.

7. Identify John Holbrook.
    He met Kit on the boat to Wethersfield. He was on his way to study to be a clergyman with Rev. Bulkeley.

8. Why did Goodwife Cruff think Kit was a witch?
    Kit could swim. According to the water trials for witches, only witches would stay afloat in water.

9. Identify Prudence.
    Prudence was Goodwife Cruff's daughter, who lost her doll in the water.

10. Why did Kit live with her grandfather in Barbados?
    Her parents were killed when she was a very little girl. He was her nearest relative.

11. Why was John surprised that Kit read plays?
    The Puritans believed that the only purpose for reading was to improve one's sinful nature. Reading plays for enjoyment was considered sinful.

12. Why weren't Kit's relatives at the dock to meet her?
>She had not told them that she was coming.

13. What was Kit's feeling about Wethersfield?
>She thought it was lonely, muddy and dull.

14. Why was Kit's grandfather no longer wealthy?
>His plantation manager sold his crop and ran off with the money. By the time of the grandfather's death, there were many bills to be paid. The land, slaves and all the household goods had to be sold to pay the debts.

15. Describe Matthew Wood.
>He is a stern, strict, serious man who believes in law and order and the Puritan way of life.

Chapters 4-7

1. What kind of a woman is Rachel?
>She is a loving, caring, truly good woman. She tends to those who are less fortunate than herself and tries to carry out her duties as a Puritan woman in the best way she knows how. She has more compassion than Goodwife Cruff or Matthew Wood.

2. What was wrong with Mercy?
>She had been left crippled by a childhood disease.

3. How did Matthew Wood react to Kit's giving clothes to his daughters?
>He was furious. He demanded that they be returned at once and ordered Kit to clean up her mess.

4. Why did Kit have to come to Connecticut?
>A marriage had been arranged for her in Barbados, but she couldn't stand the possibilities of being married to an old man.

5. What did Judith think of Kit?
>Judith took a disliking to Kit primarily because Kit couldn't help with the chores very well. Actually, considering Judith's personality, she probably had her nose out of joint because she was not the center of attention anymore and Kit had such beautiful clothes.

6. What are Sabbath houses?
>They are places where people who live far away from the meeting house can go to have lunch between the services.

7. What did Kit think of the church services?
    She detested them. They were long and boring, and she was uncomfortable there.

8. Why did Dr. Bulkeley think Matthew was a traitor?
    Matthew did not like the King's appointed governor.

9. Identify William Ashby.
    William Ashby was the eligible bachelor in the community. Judith had her sights set on him, but William took a shine to Kit when she arrived.

10. Was Judith upset about the loss of William?
    She said she wasn't, but that was probably a cover-up. She said that she wished to marry John Holbrook instead.

11. Describe William's "call" on Kit.
    His visit was extremely dull and awkward until John Holbrook came and Aunt Rachel made popcorn.

12. Why was the fact that William had started building his house significant?
    It meant that he had decided to get married; he had chosen his bride.

Chapters 8-10
1. Describe Kit's feelings about the meadows.
    She loved being in the meadows; they were beautiful and made her feel calm and comforted.

2. Identify Hannah Tupper.
    Hannah was a widow who lived alone near the meadow and the pond. Everyone believed she was a witch because she was a Quaker. She was Kit's friend as well as Nat's.

3. What job was Kit offered?
    She was asked to teach at the dame school.

4. What had happened to Mercy's brothers?
    One had died of a childhood illness. The other was born prematurely and died a short time later.

5. Why did Matthew Wood change after the death of his second son?
    Perhaps he felt responsible for the child's death since he insisted that the child would be taken to church even though he was a newborn baby and even though the weather was exceptionally cold and bad.

6. What did Kit do to anger the schoolmasters?
    She had the children act out a Bible story.

7. Where did Kit go after she had been dismissed as a teacher?
    She went to the meadow where she met Hannah, who comforted her.

8. Why did Kit go to see Mr. Kimberly?
    She went to apologize and to try to get her job back.

9. Who was Hannah's seafaring friend?
    Nat Eaton was her friend.

Chapters 11-13

1. Who left Kit flowers?
    Prudence Cruff left flowers for Kit.

2. Why didn't Prudence go to school?
    Goodwife Cruff said Prudence was too stupid and too big to go to school.

3. How did Kit teach Prudence to read?
    She met Prudence at the meadow (and at Hannah's house) and gave her lessons from a small hornbook.

4. What secret did Kit discover about Mercy?
    She could tell by Mercy's looks that Mercy was in love with John Holbrook.

5. What did Nat and Kit do for Hannah?
    Nat cut firewood for her, and he and Kit made a new roof for her house.

6. To what did Nat compare Kit?
    He compared her to a yellow-green tropical bird with scarlet patches. He said that had the bird been brought to New England, the other birds there would scold and peck at it.

7. What did Matthew Wood do when he discovered that Kit had been seeing and helping Hannah Tupper?
    He was terribly angry and told Kit that she was forbidden to see Hannah anymore.

8. Which Wood girl did John Holbrook like?
    He liked Mercy.

9. What did Judith think John was going to say?
    She thought that he was going to ask her to marry him.

10. What was Kit's response to William's marriage proposal?
    She said that she needed time to think about it.

Chapters 14-16

1. Where did Kit see Nat?
    She saw him at the harbor.

2. How did Kit feel about Governor Andros?
    She thought he was a true gentleman. People had no cause do dislike him.

3. Why was the charter safe?
    Someone had taken it away from the governor.

4. What happened to William's new home?
    A group of men illuminated it on Halloween.

5. Who was one of the men who took part in the illumination of William's home?
    Nat Eaton was one of the culprits.

6. What was Nat's punishment?
    He was put into the stocks in the square and was then banished from Wethersfield.

7. What did Kit teach Prudence to do (other than to read)?
    Kit taught Prudence to write.

8. Where did John go?
    He went off to join the militia to fight.

Chapters 17-18

1. What happened to Judith?
    She fell ill with a fever.

2. How did Mercy react to becoming sick?
    She was embarrassed. She hated causing trouble and having a fuss made over her.

3. What was Dr. Bulkeley's cure for the fever?
    He suggested putting warm onions on the ill person's chest.

4. Where did Kit hide Hannah?
   She hid her in *The Dolphin*.

5. Why did the people want Hannah?
   They wanted to kill her because they thought she used a spell to cause the illness which was spreading over the town.

6. What made Kit feel guilty?
   She felt guilty because she thought she had not done her share of the work.

7. How did the townspeople suppose Hannah had escaped?
   They thought she had changed herself into a mouse.

8. What happened to Kit?
   She was also accused of being a witch because she was known to be a friend to Hannah Tupper. Kit was locked in a shed until her hearing.

<u>Chapters 19-21</u>
1. What evidence did Goodman Cruff bring forth at the hearing?
   He produced the little copy book in which Prudence had copied her name.

2. How was Kit proved to be innocent?
   Nat brought Prudence to the hearing. She testified that Kit had taught her to read and write, and that she could read Bible stories.

3. What change came over Goodman Cruff when he found out that Prudence could read and write?
   He was very proud of Prudence. He became very brave and stood up to his wife. Goodman Cruff withdrew the charges against Kit.

4. What did John do when he got home?
   He put his head in Mercy's lap and let his true feelings be known.

5. Why had William stayed away during Kit's arrest and hearing?
   He said he stayed away in respect of the illness, but really he didn't want to be seen in Kit's company.

6. Who was going to be married?
   Judith and William were going to be married as were Mercy and John.

7. How was Kit going to afford passage back to Barbados?
   She was going to sell her beautiful clothes.

8. Who did Kit realize she loved?
    She loved Nat, and Nat loved her.

9. What did Nat buy?
    He bought a new ship and named it *The Witch*, for Kit.

MULTIPLE CHOICE STUDY GUIDE/QUIZ QUESTIONS - *The Witch of Blackbird Pond*

Chapters 1-3

1. Where did Kit live before going on this journey?
    a. She lived in Barbados.
    b. She lived in England.
    c. She lived in Connecticut.
    d. She lived in Mexico.

2. Where did Mistress Eaton spend her summers?
    a. She spent summers on her son's ship.
    b. She spent summers at home in Saybrook, tending her garden.
    c. She spent summers in Boston visiting her sister.
    d. She spent summers in the West Indies.

3. What was a new sensation for Kit?
    a. Cold was a new sensation.
    b. Embarrassment was a new sensation.
    c. Fright was a new sensation.
    d. Anger was a new sensation.

4. Why did Kit jump off the longboat?
    a. She had left her hat and suitcase on the wharf.
    b. She was suddenly afraid to go on with the journey, and she wanted to stay with Mistress Eaton.
    c. A little girl had lost her doll in the water, and the captain wouldn't turn around to get it.
    d. She loved to swim and just decided to get some exercise.

5. Who is Goodwife Cruff?
    a. She was the sister of Mistress Eaton, and had offered to look after Kit on the rest of the journey.
    b. She was the captain's wife. She was interested in getting to know more about Kit's former life.
    c. She was the wife of the town's minister. She thought she was responsible for encouraging proper behavior in all of the townspeople.
    d. She was the somber mother of a little girl on the ship.

6. How did people react when Kit said she could swim?
    a. They were impressed and wanted her to teach them.
    b. They were surprised and suspicious.
    TWO CHOICES ONLY

23

The Witch of Blackbird Pond Multiple Choice Questions Page 2

7. Who was John Holbrook?
    a. He was a passenger on the ship. He was on his way to study to be a clergyman with Reverend Bulkeley.
    b. He was the first mate on the ship.
    c. He was a merchant traveling on the ship. He had been to Kit's homeland several times, and they talked about this extensively.
    d. He was the owner of the ship. He was developing an interest in Kit.

8. True or False: Goodwife Cruff thought Kit was a witch because Kit could swim. According to the water trials for witches, only witches would stay afloat in water.
    a. True
    b. False

9. Who was Prudence?
    a. She was a young widow who was also traveling on the ship.
    b. She was the captain's mother, who was staying on the ship for a visit with him.
    c. She was Goodwife Cruff's daughter.
    d. She was John Holbrook's sister-in-law, who was traveling with him.

10. Why had Kit lived with her grandfather?
    a. Her parents could not afford to keep her, and they sent her to live with him.
    b. Her parents were killed when she was very young. He was her nearest relative.
    c. Her parents were missionaries. They left her with him when they went to India, but they had never returned.
    d. He was old and needed company and someone to take care of him. He paid Kit's parents a large sum of money for the assistance.

11. What about Kit's reading surprised John?
    a. He was surprised that she could read at all, because none of the other women he knew could read.
    b. She owned her own collection of books, and he had never met anyone before who owned more than a Bible.
    c. She was reading plays, which was considered sinful.
    d. She was able to read Latin and Greek as well as English.

The Witch of Blackbird Pond Multiple Choice Questions Page 3

12. Why weren't Kit's relatives at the dock to meet her?
    a. They believed it was a waste of time to leave their work when she could find her own way to their house.
    b. They had been told the wrong day of arrival for the ship. They thought it was coming in the following week.
    c. They were all sick and were not able to leave their houses.
    d. They didn't know she was coming.

13. True or False: Kit thought Wethersfield was lonely, muddy and dull.
    a. True
    b. False

14. Why was Kit's grandfather no longer wealthy?
    a. The country had been taken over by a new government, who had confiscated all property and money from the wealthy landowners.
    b. He had lost his money because of a few bad business deals.
    c. The plantation manager had sold the crop and run off with the money.
    d. There had been several severe hurricanes which had destroyed the crops.

15. True or False: Matthew Wood was religious, but was still able to see other people's viewpoints, and believed in letting others think for themselves.
    a. True
    b. False

The Witch of Blackbird Pond Multiple Choice Questions Page 4

Chapters 4-7

16. True of False: Rachel is a loving, caring, truly good woman. She tends to those who are less fortunate and tries to carry out her duties as a Puritan woman in the best way she knows how.
    a. True
    b. False

17. What was wrong with Mercy?
    a. She had been born prematurely and had not developed correctly.
    b. She had been struck by lightning.
    c. She had been crippled by a childhood disease.
    d. She had fallen off of a roof and there was not doctor to set her leg, so it had healed incorrectly.

18. How did Matthew Wood react to Kit's giving clothes to his daughters?
    a. He was pleased.
    b. He was appreciative, but insisted on paying for them.
    c. He was furious. He demanded that they be returned at once.
    d. He felt badly that he wasn't able to provide for his own daughters and wife.

19. True or False: Kit came to Connecticut to escape a marriage that had been arranged for her.
    a. True
    b. False

20. What did Judith think of Kit?
    a. She liked Kit very much, and admired her bravery.
    b. She disliked Kit because Kit would not help with the chores and she had beautiful clothes.
    TWO CHOICES ONLY

21. What were the places called where people who lived far away from the meeting house could go to have lunch between the services?
    a. They were called taverns.
    b. They were called sanctuaries.
    c. They were called Sabbath houses.
    d. They were called rest havens.

22. What did kit think of the church services?
    a. She detested them. She thought they were long and boring.
    b. She enjoyed the solemnity and ritual.
    TWO CHOICES ONLY

The Witch of Blackbird Pond Multiple Choice Questions Page 5

23. Why did Dr. Bulkeley think Matthew was a traitor?
    a. He believed in slavery.
    b. He thought all men should be allowed to worship as they pleased.
    c. He did not like the King's appointed governor.
    d. He thought the colonies should be free from rule by England.

24. Who was William Ashby?
    a. He was the new governor.
    b. He was the town elder.
    c. He was the eligible bachelor in the community.
    d. He was Matthew Wood's cousin who had come to visit.

25. How did Judith feel about the loss of William?
    a. She was glad, because she never liked him anyway.
    b. She was upset, because she had hoped to marry him.
    TWO CHOICES ONLY

26. True or False: William's visit to Kit was very lively until John Holbrook came and put everyone in a somber mood.
    a. True
    b. False

27. Why was the fact that William had started building his house significant?
    a. It meant that the town was going to expand.
    b. It meant that his father was about to die, and William would be left on his own.
    c. It meant that the lumber business was good, and there would be plenty of jobs for the men.
    d. It meant that he had decided to get married, and had chosen his bride.

The Witch of Blackbird Pond Multiple Choice Questions Page 6

<u>Chapters 8-10</u>

28. How did Kit feel about the meadows?
    a. She loved being there; they were beautiful and made her feel calm and comforted.
    b. She didn't like them. The grasses made her sneeze and itch.
    TWO CHOICES ONLY

29. Which of the following does not describe Hannah Tupper?
    a. She was a widow who lived alone.
    b. She was a Quaker.
    c. She was secretly wealthy.
    d. She was Nat's friend.

30. What job was Kit offered?
    a. She was asked to be companion for the minister's wife.
    b. She was asked to work in the general store.
    c. She was asked to become a nurse.
    d. She was asked to teach at the dame school.

31. What had happened to Mercy's brothers?
    a. They had both run off to join the sea merchants.
    b. One had been killed by Indians; and the other had died of pneumonia.
    c. One had died of a childhood illness. The other had been born prematurely and had died a short time later.
    d. They both lived in the neighboring town, although they seldom came home. The second son had been disowned by his father, and the older brother stood by him.

32. True or False: Matthew Wood felt responsible for what had happened to his second son.
    a. True
    b. False

33. What did Kit do to anger the schoolmasters?
    a. She read poetry to the children.
    b. She taught them to draw pictures of happy things.
    c. She had them act out a Bible story.
    d. She allowed the children to have recess.

The Witch of Blackbird Pond Multiple Choice Questions Page 7

34. Where did Kit go after she had been dismissed as a teacher?
    a. She went to the river for a swim.
    b. She went to the church.
    c. She went to her aunt's house.
    d. She went to the meadow where she met Hannah.

35. Why did Kit go to see Mr. Kimberly?
    a. She went to demand her pay.
    b. She went to apologize and try to get her job back.
    c. She went to recommend Mercy for the position.
    d. She went to tell him exactly what she thought of him.

36. Who was Hannah's friend?
    a. It was William Ashby.
    b. It was Matthew Wood.
    c. It was John Holbrook.
    d. It was Nat Eaton.

The Witch of Blackbird Pond Multiple Choice Questions Page 8

Chapters 11-13

37. Who left flowers for Kit?
    a. It was Nat Eaton.
    b. It was Hannah.
    c. It was Prudence Cruff.
    d. It was William.

38. Why didn't Prudence go to school?
    a. She was needed at home to care for the younger children.
    b. Her mother said she was too stupid and too big to go to school.
    c. Her father didn't think book learning was important for a girl.
    d. She was afraid to leave her home and interact with other children.

39. How did Kit teach Prudence to read?
    a. She wrote letters to Prudence and helped her read them.
    b. She used her book of plays and had Prudence read aloud with her.
    c. She wrote words in the dirt with a stick.
    d. She met Prudence in the meadow and gave her lessons from a small hornbook.

40. What secret did Kit discover about Mercy?
    a. She was probably going to die within the next six months.
    b. She was in love with John Holbrook.
    c. She could really walk but didn't want to tell anyone.
    d. She was planning to run away and live in Boston.

41. What did Nat and Kit do for Hannah?
    a. They cut firewood and made a new roof for her house.
    b. They harvested the vegetables from her garden.
    c. They built a new room onto her house.
    d. They took her shopping in town.

42. To what did Nat compare Kit?
    a. He compared her to the morning sunshine.
    b. He compared her to a dolphin.
    c. He compared her to a yellow-green tropical bird with scarlet patches.
    d. He compared her to his ship.

The Witch of Blackbird Pond Multiple Choice Questions Page 9

43. What did Matthew Wood do when he discovered that Kit had been seeing and helping Hannah Tupper?
    a. He commended her for her generosity.
    b. He was angry and told Kit she was forbidden to see Hannah any more.
    TWO CHOICES ONLY

44. Whom did John Holbrook like?
    a. He liked Kit.
    b. He didn't like any of them.
    c. He liked Mercy.
    d. He liked Judith.

45. True or False: Judith thought John was going to ask her to marry him?
    a. True
    b. False

46. What was Kit's response to William's marriage proposal?
    a. She readily accepted.
    b. She said that she needed time to think about it.
    c. She refused him on the spot.
    THREE CHOICES ONLY

The Witch of Blackbird Pond Multiple Choice Questions Page 10

Chapters 14-16

47. Where did Kit see Nat?

    a. She saw him at church.

    b. He came to visit her at the Wood's home.

    c. She saw him at the harbor.

    d. She met him in the meadow.

48. How did Kit feel about Governor Andros?

    a. She thought he was a true gentlemen, and that people had no cause to dislike him.

    b. She thought he was unpleasant and not at all likeable.

    TWO CHOICES ONLY

49. Why was the charter safe?

    a. The King had the original copy.

    b. The governor had committed it to memory.

    c. The minister was keeping it.

    d. It had been taken away from the governor.

50. When did the group of men illuminate William's new home?

    a. It was on the night of the Winter Solstice.

    b. It was on Halloween.

    c. It was on Christmas Eve.

    d. It was on William's birthday.

51. Who was one of the men who took part in the illumination?

    a. John Holbrook was one of the culprits.

    b. Matthew Wood was one of the culprits.

    c. Nat Eaton was one of the culprits.

    d. Mr. Cruff was one of the culprits.

52. What was the participant's punishment?

    a. He received fifty lashes.

    b. He was fined the cost of repairing the house.

    c. He was made to apologize publicly and complete the repairs himself.

    d. He was put into the stocks in the square and then banished from Wethersfield.

The Witch of Blackbird Pond Multiple Choice Questions Page 11

53. What did Kit teach Prudence to do (other than to read)?
    a. Kit taught her to sing.
    b. Kit taught her to swim.
    c. Kit taught her to write.
    d. Kit taught her to climb trees.

54. Where did John go?
    a. He went to Boston to study at the Harvard School of Divinity.
    b. He went off to join the militia to fight.
    c. He went to become a missionary in India.
    d. He went to live in a neighboring town.

The Witch of Blackbird Pond Multiple Choice Questions Page 12

Chapters 17-18

55. What happened to Judith?
    a. She fell and broke her leg.
    b. She became depressed over losing John.
    c. She spilled a kettle of boiling water on her arm.
    d. She fell ill with fever.

56. How did Mercy react to being sick?
    a. She was embarrassed. She hated causing trouble and having a fuss made over her.
    b. She accepted it stoically.
    c. She became irritable and demanding.
    d. She became very scared, and cried almost constantly.

57. What was Dr. Bulkeley's cure for the fever?
    a. He suggested bleeding the patient.
    b. He suggested putting the patient in a tub of very cold water.
    c. He suggested putting warm onions on the ill person's chest.
    d. He said the only remedy was prayer.

58. Where did Kit hide Hannah?
    a. She hid her in the Wood's barn.
    b. She hid her in the Dolphin.
    c. She hid her in her own attic.
    d. She hid her in a closet at the church.

59. True or False: The people wanted Hannah because they thought she knew a remedy for the illness.
    a. True
    b. False

60. How did Kit feel?
    a. She felt resentful that she had to do so much work.
    b. She felt guilty that she had not done her share of the work.
    TWO CHOICES ONLY

The Witch of Blackbird Pond Multiple Choice Questions Page 13

61. How did the townspeople suppose Hannah had escaped?
    a. They thought she had changed herself into a fish and had escaped by the river.
    b. They thought she had changed herself into a bird and had flown away.
    c. They thought she had made herself invisible and was still among them.
    d. They thought she had changed herself into a mouse and had run away.

62. True or False: Kit was also accused of being a witch because she was known to be a friend of Hannah's?
    a. True
    b. False

The Witch of Blackbird Pond Multiple Choice Questions Page 14

Chapters 19-21

63. What evidence did Goodman Cruff Bring forth at the hearing?
    a. He said he had heard Prudence talking about casting spells she had learned from Kate.
    b. He showed the people a gold coin that Kit had given to Prudence.
    c. He brought a small bundle of things that Prudence had tied in a handkerchief. The bundle contained a lock of hair, a bird's feather, some grass, and two pebbles. He thought they were evil talismans.
    d. He produced the little copy book in which Prudence had copied her name.

64. True or False: Kit was proven innocent by Prudence's testimony and demonstration of her reading and writing abilities.
    a. True
    b. False

65. Some changes came over Goodman Cruff when he discovered Prudence's abilities. Which of the following was not one of the changes?
    a. He became proud of Prudence.
    b. He dropped to his knees and declared that God had caused a miracle.
    c. He became brave and stood up to his wife.
    d. He withdrew the charges.

66. What did John do when he got home?
    a. He locked himself in his room to pray.
    b. He busied himself cleaning.
    c. He put his head on Mercy's lap and let his true feelings be known.
    d. He announced that he was leaving the area.

67. True or False: William had stayed away during Kit's arrest and trial because he had been ill.
    a. True
    b. False

68. Who was going to be married?
    a. Kit and William were going to be married, as were Mercy and John.
    b. Judith and William were going to be married, as were Kit and John.
    c. Judith and William were going to be married, as were Mercy and John.
    d. Kit and Nat were going to be married, as were Mercy and William.

The Witch of Blackbird Pond Multiple Choice Questions Page 15

69. How was Kit going to afford passage back to Barbados?
- a. Matthew Wood gave her the money, and she said she would repay it after she arrived back in Barbados.
- b. Nat gave her the money.
- c. She was going to teach for a few months and use the salary for passage.
- d. She was going to sell her beautiful clothes.

70. What did Kit realize?
- a. She realized that she wanted to convert to the Quaker way of life.
- b. She realized that she loved Nat, and he loved her.
- c. She realized she was very angry for the way the people in Wethersfield had treated her.
- d. She realized that she had no feelings at all for her relatives.

71. What did Nat buy?
- a. He bought a house in the village.
- b. He bought a new dress for Hannah.
- c. He bought the meadow that Kit liked so much.
- d. He bought a new ship and named it *The Witch*, for Kit.

ANSWER KEY - MULTIPLE CHOICE STUDY/QUIZ QUESTIONS
The Witch of Blackbird Pond

Chapters 1-3	Chapters 4-7	Chapters 8-10	Chapters 11-13
1. A	16. A	28. A	37. C
2. B	17. C	29. C	38. B
3. B	18. C	30. D	39. D
4. C	19. A	31. C	40. B
5. D	20. B	32. A	41. A
6. B	21. C	33. C	42. C
7. A	22. A	34. D	43. B
8. A	23. C	35. B	44. C
9. C	24. D	36. D	45. A
10. B	25. B		46. B
11. C	26. B		
12. D	27. D		
13. A			
14. C			
15. B			

Chapters 14-16	Chapters 17-18	Chapters 19-21
47. C	55. D	63. D
48. A	56. A	64. A
49. D	57. C	65. B
50. B	58. B	66. C
51. C	59. B	67. B
52. D	60. B	68. C
53. C	61. D	69. D
54. B	62. A	70. B
		71. D

PREREADING VOCABULARY WORKSHEETS

VOCABULARY - *The Witch of Blackbird Pond*

<u>Chapters 1-3</u> Part I: Using Prior Knowledge and Contextual Clues

Below are the sentences in which the vocabulary words appear in the text. Read the sentence. Use any clues you can find in the sentence combined with your prior knowledge, and write what you think the underlined words mean on the lines provided.

1. Kit greeted her <u>wistfully</u>.

_____

2. They were halfway across the harbor when a wail of <u>anguish</u> broke from the child.

_____

3. When a thin whimper from the child was silenced by a vicious <u>cuff</u>, her anger boiled over.

_____

4. "You must be <u>daft</u>," the woman hissed.

_____

5. She had made them both laugh, but underneath her <u>nonchalance</u>, Kit felt uneasy.

_____

6. Once or twice she had seen the father <u>furtively</u> slip the child an extra morsel from his plate, but he was plainly too spineless to stand up for her against his shrew of a wife.

_____

7. Captain Eaton treated her with <u>punctilious</u> caution.

_____

8. Painfully, almost <u>imperceptibly</u>, the *Dolphin* inched forward through the water.

_____

Vocabulary - *The Witch of Blackbird Pond* Chapters 1-3 Continued

9. All the same, the <u>reproof</u> in John Holbrook's voice left her discomforted.

_____

Part II: Determining the Meaning - Match the vocabulary words to their dictionary definitions.

___ 1. wistfully   A. done or acting in a stealthy way; sneaky
___ 2. anguish   B. very careful about every detail of behavior
___ 3. cuff   C. longing pensively; expressing vague yearnings
___ 4. daft   D. gradually, slightly, so as to be difficult to perceive
___ 5. nonchalance   E. rebuke; censure; find fault with
___ 6. furtively   F. great suffering as from worry, grief or pain
___ 7. punctilious   G. to strike with open hand; a slap or blow
___ 8. imperceptibly   H. showing cool lack of concern
___ 9. reproof   I. silly; foolish; insane; crazy

Vocabulary - *The Witch of Blackbird Pond*   Chapters 4-7

Part I: Using Prior Knowledge and Contextual Clues
   Below are the sentences in which the vocabulary words appear in the text. Read the sentence. Use any clues you can find in the sentence combined with your prior knowledge, and write what you think the underlined words mean on the lines provided.

10. Kit felt a surge of generosity that was new and <u>exhilarating</u>.

_____

11. Judith was not so easily <u>intimidated</u>.

_____

12. Surprise and <u>chagrin</u> left Kit speechless.

_____

13. Her stirring became more and more halfhearted till Judith snatched the stick in <u>exasperation</u>.

_____

14. The smoke made her eyes water, and there was a smarting blister on one thumb. She suspected that Judith had invented the <u>irksome</u> procedure just to keep her busy. . . . .

_____

15. But the greatest part of his <u>condescension</u> he had bestowed on Kit, once he had understood that her grandfather had been Sir Francis Tyler.

_____

16. As the husky voice scraped <u>inexorably</u> on, she ventured to raise her head a little, and was gratified to see that Judith too was peeking.

_____

43

Vocabulary - *The Witch of Blackbird Pond* Chapters 4-7 Continued

17. She coaxed her father out of his bitter moods, upheld her <u>timorous</u> and anxious mother, gently restrained her rebellious sister and had reached to draw an uncertain alien into the circle.

_____

18. A shearing had brought a <u>veritable</u> mountain of gray wool to be washed and bleached and dyed, enough to keep Mercy carding and spinning and weaving for the next twelve months.

_____

Part II: Determining the Meaning - Match the vocabulary words to their dictionary definitions.

___ 10. exhilarating   A. mortification; a feeling of embarrassment
___ 11. intimidated   B. tiresome; annoying; irritating
___ 12. chagrin   C. invigorating or stimulating
___ 13. exasperation   D. made afraid; made timid; cowed
___ 14. irksome   E. timid; full of or subject to fear
___ 15. condescension   F. unrelentingly; cannot be stopped
___ 16. inexorably   G. a patronizing manner or behavior
___ 17. timorous   H. in fact; actual; truly
___ 18. veritable   I. a state of being vexed, irritated or annoyed

Vocabulary - *The Witch of Blackbird Pond* Chapters 8-10

Part I: Using Prior Knowledge and Contextual Clues

    Below are the sentences in which the vocabulary words appear in the text. Read the sentence. Use any clues you can find in the sentence combined with your prior knowledge, and write what you think the underlined words mean on the lines provided.

19. While Kit resorted to <u>ingenious</u> tricks, Mercy possessed the patience.

_____

20. The children were <u>entranced</u>.

_____

21. Out from behind the settle popped the robbers, and set upon him with a <u>vengeance</u>.

_____

22. Such an opportunity, <u>sanctioned</u> by authority, had never been known before.

_____

23. When the talk turned to politics, as it <u>invariably</u> did, William made a far better showing than John.

_____

24. The <u>vagueness</u> was gone as suddenly as it had come.

_____

Vocabulary - *The Witch of Blackbird Pond* Chapters 8-10 Continued

Part II: Determining the Meaning

Match the vocabulary words to their dictionary definitions. If there are words for which you cannot figure out the definition by contextual clues and by process of elimination, look them up in a dictionary.

___ 19. ingenious
___ 20. entranced
___ 21. vengeance
___ 22. sanctioned
___ 23. invariably
___ 24. vagueness

A. not changing; constant
B. with great force or fury; excessively; revenge
C. fill with rapture or delight; enchant; charm
D. not clearly; hazily; obscurely; not sharp
E. clever; resourceful; original and inventive
F. authorized approval or permission

Vocabulary - *The Witch of Blackbird Pond* Chapters 11-13

Part I: Using Prior Knowledge and Contextual Clues

Below are the sentences in which the vocabulary words appear in the text. Read the sentence. Use any clues you can find in the sentence combined with your prior knowledge, and write what you think the underlined words mean on the lines provided.

25. Here in New England books contained only a dreary collection of sermons, or at most some pious religious poetry.

___

26. She had a feeling that the child needed that comforting refuge even more than she did herself.

___

27. The bony hand in hers was trembling as they walked down the grassy path, but Prudence stepped resolutely beside her.

___

28. Kit shook off her qualms and set her own face towards home and another dull evening.

___

29. Kit was in a mood to overlook his mockery.

___

30. In spite of the fact that he was often bewildered and scandalized, he was still as infatuated as he had been that first Sabbath morning.

___

31. Judith tipped back her head and smiled up at him provocatively.

___

32. "Oh, Father!" she cried impetuously.

___

Vocabulary - *The Witch of Blackbird Pond* Chapters 11-13 Continued

33. Then, still <u>incredulous</u>, he looked back at Judith.

_____

Part II: Determining the Meaning - Match the vocabulary words to their dictionary definitions.

___ 25. pious
___ 26. refuge
___ 27. resolutely
___ 28. qualms
___ 29. mockery
___ 30. infatuated
___ 31. provocatively
___ 32. impetuously
___ 33. incredulous

A. feeling of uneasiness or doubt; misgiving
B. tending to provoke as to action, thought or feeling
C. doubting; skeptical; unwilling or unable to believe
D. seemingly virtuous; showing religious devotion
E. ridicule; false, derisive or impertinent imitation
F. rash; impulsive; done suddenly with little thought
G. a place of safety
H. showing a fixed, firm purpose; determined; faithful
I. carried away by shallow love or affection; foolish

Vocabulary - *The Witch of Blackbird Pond* Chapters 14-16

Part I: Using Prior Knowledge and Contextual Clues
Below are the sentences in which the vocabulary words appear in the text. Read the sentence. Use any clues you can find in the sentence combined with your prior knowledge, and write what you think the underlined words mean on the lines provided.

34. Kit was thankful when she and Judith could escape to the cold sanctuary of the upstairs....

_____

35. The Colony of Connecticut is annexed to Massachusetts.

_____

36. All Saints' Day is a papist feast.

_____

37. 'Twas an outrageous piece of blasphemy.

_____

38. She could not face the family, or the whispering and staring that would turn her own family pew into a pillory.

_____

39. Hannah ruefully surveyed the length of gray woolen.

_____

40. Then Prudence and I will make you a dress," promised Kit blithely.

_____

41. From her pocket she drew three precious objects that had required some ingenuity to gather, a partly used copybook from her trunk, a small bottle of ink, and a quill pen.

_____

Witch of Blackbird Pond Vocabulary Chapters 14-16 Continued

42. Was there some premonition, she would wonder, that made that moment so <u>poignant</u>, some foreknowledge that this was the last afternoon the three would ever spend together ... ?

_____

Part II: Determining the Meaning - Match the vocabulary words to their dictionary definitions.

____ 34. sanctuary
____ 35. annexed
____ 36. papist
____ 37. blasphemy
____ 38. pillory
____ 39. ruefully
____ 40. blithely
____ 41. ingenuity
____ 42. poignant

A. to add on or attach; append
B. cleverness, originality, skill; ingeniousness
C. a place of refuge or protection; a holy place for worship
D. emotionally touching or moving; pungent smell or taste
E. feeling or showing regret; lamentable; mournful
F. showing a gay, cheerful disposition; carefree
G. contemptuous speech or action concerning God
H. Roman Catholic; one who believes in papal supremacy
I. a wooden device with holes for head and hands into which petty offenders were locked and exposed to public ridicule

Vocabulary - *The Witch of Blackbird Pond* Chapters 17 and 18

Part I: Using Prior Knowledge and Contextual Clues

Below are the sentences in which the vocabulary words appear in the text. Read the sentence. Use any clues you can find in the sentence combined with your prior knowledge, and write what you think the underlined words mean on the lines provided.

43. The three women's eyes met in consternation.

_____

44. "His judgment on us for harboring an infidel and a Quaker.

_____

45. She could hear a man's voice across the water, but the fog rolled tantalizingly between her and the ship.

_____

46. Still dazed, Hannah accepted the miracle and the prospect of a journey like a docile child.

_____

47. Kit could have laughed out loud, but a look at Goodwife Cruff sobered her.

_____

48. Sustained by her aunt's visit, Kit was able to face the morrow with less panic.

_____

49. Who had inveigled the child with promises, and thought of the hiding place under the willow tree, and persuaded her--no dragged her against her will--to meet Hannah?

_____

Witch of Blackbird Pond Vocabulary Chapters 17-18 Continued

Part II: Determining the Meaning - Match the vocabulary words to their dictionary definitions.

___ 43. consternation
___ 44. infidel
___ 45. tantalizingly
___ 46. docile
___ 47. sobered
___ 48. sustained
___ 49. inveigled

A. easy to manage or discipline; obedient; teachable
B. led by deception; enticed or tricked into something
C. great fear or shock that makes one feel helpless
D. strengthened in spirit or courage; kept up; maintained
E. one who does not believe in a particular religion
F. teasing by keeping out of reach something desirable
G. characterized by reason, sanity, or self-control

Vocabulary - *The Witch of Blackbird Pond* Chapters 19-21

Part I: Using Prior Knowledge and Contextual Clues
Below are the sentences in which the vocabulary words appear in the text. Read the sentence. Use any clues you can find in the sentence combined with your prior knowledge, and write what you think the underlined words mean on the lines provided.

50. Benches and chairs along the two walls were crowded with men from the town, with here and there a sharp-faced woman, cronies of Goodwife Cruff.

_____

51. For the last few moments Goodwife Cruff had been vehemently prodding her husband.

_____

52. "Seven different kinds of cake," Judith counted surreptitiously.

_____

53. In some contradictory way grief seemed to have etched on Mercy's face a beauty it had never possessed.

_____

54. She resented the arduous preparation for the journey to Meeting, the heavy leather boots, the knit socks drawn over them, the clumsy little footstove they had to lug all the way, that cooled off long before the sermon was finished and left one to sit with stinging fingers and toes, while the breath of the whole congregation rose like the smoke from so many pipes.

_____

55. No, she amended, Judith would never be a spinster.

_____

56. There was the vital matter of two dowries.

_____

Witch of Blackbird Pond Vocabulary Chapters 19-21 Continued

57. His words came in an <u>unpremeditated</u> rush.

_____

Part II: Determining the Meaning - Match the vocabulary words to their dictionary definitions.

___ 50. cronies
___ 51. vehemently
___ 52. surreptitiously

___ 53. contradictory
___ 54. arduous
___ 55. amended
___ 56. dowries
___ 57. unpremeditated

A. asserting the opposite of what someone else said
B. in a secret, stealthy way; clandestine
C. the property a woman brings to her husband at marriage
D. done without any plan or forethought
E. difficult to do; laborious; strenuous
F. impassioned; fervent; impetuous
G. old friends; close companions
H. made better, changed or revised

ANSWER KEY - VOCABULARY
The Witch of Blackbird Pond

Chapters 1-3	Chapters 4-7	Chapters 8-10	Chapters 11-13
1. C	10. C	19. E	25. D
2. F	11. D	20. C	26. G
3. G	12. A	21. B	27. H
4. I	13. I	22. F	28. A
5. H	14. B	23. A	29. E
6. A	15. G	24. D	30. I
7. B	16. F		31. B
8. D	17. E		32. F
9. E	18. H		33. C

Chapters 14-16	Chapters 17-18	Chapters 19-21
34. C	43. C	50. G
35. A	44. E	51. F
36. H	45. F	52. B
37. G	46. A	53. A
38. I	47. G	54. E
39. E	48. D	55. H
40. F	49. B	56. C
41. B		57. D
42. D		

DAILY LESSONS

LESSON ONE

Objectives
    1. To introduce *The Witch of Blackbird Pond* unit.
    2. To distribute books and other related materials
    3. To preview the study questions for chapters 1-3
    4. To familiarize students with the vocabulary for chapters 1-3
    5. To read chapters 1-3

Activity #1

    Do a little travelogue about Barbados and the islands. Perhaps your local travel agent would have a video you could show. If not, try a large video store in your area; they sometimes carry travelogue videos.

    Transition: Ask students what their impressions are of Puritan New England. Give them ample time to answer. Then, ask them how they think one would feel going from Barbados to Puritan New England. Allow ample time for answers. Explain that the heroine of the book they are about to read had to do just that.

    Alternate Introductory Activity: If you cannot find a video about Barbados and the islands, focus on the aspect of moving to a new area. Ask how many students in your class have ever moved to a new neighborhood. Discuss how they felt about moving, what adjustments they had to make, etc. As a transition, explain that the heroine of the book they are about to read had to relocate, and she had a hard time adjusting to her new environment.

Activity #2

    Distribute the materials students will use in this unit. Explain in detail how students are to use these materials.

    Study Guides Students should read the study guide questions for each reading assignment prior to beginning the reading assignment to get a feeling for what events and ideas are important in the section they are about to read. After reading the section, students will (as a class or individually) answer the questions to review the important events and ideas from that section of the book. Students should keep the study guides as study materials for the unit test.

    Vocabulary Prior to reading a reading assignment, students will do vocabulary work related to the section of the book they are about to read. Following the completion of the reading of the book, there will be a vocabulary review of all the words used in the vocabulary assignments. Students should keep their vocabulary work as study materials for the unit test.

Reading Assignment Sheet   You need to fill in the reading assignment sheet to let students know by when their reading has to be completed. You can either write the assignment sheet up on a side blackboard or bulletin board and leave it there for students to see each day, or you can "ditto" copies for each student to have. In either case, you should advise students to become very familiar with the reading assignments so they know what is expected of them.

Extra Activities Center   The Unit Resource portion of this unit contains suggestions for an extra library of related books and articles in your classroom as well as crossword and word search puzzles. Make an extra activities center in your room where you will keep these materials for students to use. (Bring the books and articles in from the library and keep several copies of the puzzles on hand.) Explain to students that these materials are available for students to use when they finish reading assignments or other class work early.

Nonfiction Assignment Sheet   Explain to students that they each are to read at least one non-fiction piece from the in-class library at some time during the unit. Students will fill out a nonfiction assignment sheet after completing the reading to help you evaluate their reading experiences and to help the students think about and evaluate their own reading experiences.

Books   Each school has its own rules and regulations regarding student use of school books. Advise students of the procedures that are normal for your school.

Activity #3
Preview the study questions and show students how to do the vocabulary work for Chapters 1-3 of *The Witch of Blackbird Pond*. Tell students that they should have this work completed prior to your next class meeting.

NONFICTION ASSIGNMENT SHEET - *Witch of Blackbird Pond*
(To be completed after reading the required nonfiction article)

Name _____ Date _____

Title of Nonfiction Read _____

Written By _____ Publication Date _____

I. Factual Summary: Write a short summary of the piece you read.

II. Vocabulary
    1. With which vocabulary words in the piece did you encounter some degree of difficulty?

    2. How did you resolve your lack of understanding with these words?

III. Interpretation: What was the main point the author wanted you to get from reading his work?

IV. Criticism
    1. With which points of the piece did you agree or find easy to accept? Why?

    2. With which points of the piece did you disagree or find difficult to believe? Why?

V. Personal Response: What do you think about this piece? <u>OR</u> How does this piece influence your ideas?

LESSON TWO

Objectives
1. To read chapters 1-3
2. To give students practice reading orally
3. To evaluate students' oral reading

Activity

Have students read chapters 1-3 of *The Witch of Blackbird Pond* out loud in class. You probably know the best way to get readers with your class; pick students at random, ask for volunteers, or use whatever method works best for your group. If you have not yet completed an oral reading evaluation for your students this marking period, this would be a good opportunity to do so. A form is included with this unit for your convenience. If students do not complete reading chapters 1-3 in class, they should do so prior to your next class meeting.

LESSON THREE

Objectives
1. To review the main events and ideas from chapters 1-3
2. To preview the study questions for chapters 4-7
3. To familiarize students with the vocabulary in chapters 4-7
4. To read chapters 4-7

Activity #1

Give students a few minutes to formulate answers for the study guide questions for chapters 1-3, and then discuss the answers to the questions in detail. Write the answers on the board or overhead transparency so students can have the correct answers for study purposes. Note: It is a good practice in public speaking and leadership skills for individual students to take charge of leading the discussions of the study questions. Perhaps a different student could go to the front of the class and lead the discussion each day that the study questions are discussed during this unit. Of course, the teacher should guide the discussion when appropriate and be sure to fill in any gaps the students leave.

Activity #2

Give students about fifteen minutes to preview the study questions for
chapters 4-7 of *The Witch of Blackbird Pond* and to do the related vocabulary work.

Activity #3

Have students read chapters 4-7 of *The Witch of Blackbird Pond* orally in class. Continue the oral reading evaluations. If students do not complete reading chapters 4-7 in class, they should do so prior to your next class meeting.

ORAL READING EVALUATION - *The Witch of Blackbird Pond*

Name _____ Class____ Date _____

SKILL	EXCELLENT	GOOD	AVERAGE	FAIR	POOR
Fluency	5	4	3	2	1
Clarity	5	4	3	2	1
Audibility	5	4	3	2	1
Pronunciation	5	4	3	2	1
_____	5	4	3	2	1
_____	5	4	3	2	1

Total _____ Grade _____

Comments:

LESSONS FOUR AND FIVE

Objectives
    1. To review the main ideas and events from chapters 4-7
    2. To introduce the group project
    3. To preview and read chapters 8-10

Activity #1
    Give students a few minutes to formulate answers to the study questions for chapters 4-7. Discuss students' answers in detail. Write the correct answers on the board for students to copy for study use later.

Activity #2
    Tell students that prior to your next class period they should do the prereading work (previewing study questions and doing prereading vocabulary worksheet) for chapters 8-10.

Activity #3
    Divide your class into six groups. Assign one of the following topics to each group: witchcraft, Puritans, Quakers, historical background for England in the years around 1650-1700, historical background in America in the years around 1650-1700, and sailing/trade ships & shipping in 1650-1700. Distribute the Research and Report Assignment Sheet and discuss the directions in detail.

Activity #4
    Take your students to the library to do their research. You might review the places where they would be likely to find information if your class has not done research in your library this year.

RESEARCH AND REPORT ASSIGNMENT - *Witch of Blackbird Pond*

PROMPT

Your group has been assigned one of the following topics: witchcraft, Puritans, Quakers, historical background for England in the years 1650-1700, historical background for America in 1650-1700, or sailing/trade ships and shipping in 1650-1700.

Your assignment is in three parts. First, use the library/media center to gather information about your topic. Then you will get together with your group members to compile your information. Finally, you will make a presentation about your topic to the class.

GETTING STARTED

To make the best use of your time in the library, get together with the other members of your group for a few minutes to determine what aspects of your topic would be most appropriate to cover. Then, assign one aspect of your topic to each group member. Each of you, then, will have a specific research assignment to complete while you are in the library. Each of you should take notes as you do your research so you will be able to remember all the important points you have found. Fill a Nonfiction Assignment Sheet for each of the sources you use.

When you get back together as a group, each of you should explain your findings to the rest of your group. After you all have heard all of the information, work together to compile your facts into a logical presentation. Be sure to assign one portion of the presentation to each group member.

THE PRESENTATION

Finally, after your presentation is prepared, you will make that oral presentation to the class. You will be graded on the completeness of the content as well as the delivery of your presentation. Your presentation should last approximately 8-10 minutes.

LESSON SIX

Objectives
1. To review the main events and ideas from chapters 8-10
2. To preview the study questions for chapters 11-13
3. To familiarize students with the vocabulary in chapters 11-13
4. To read chapters 11-13
5. To give students the opportunity to get together in their groups to work on their presentations

Activity #1
Give students a few minutes to formulate answers for the study guide questions for chapters 8-10, and then discuss the answers to the questions in detail. Write the answers on the board or overhead transparency so students can have the correct answers for study purposes.

Activity #2
Tell students that prior to your next class meeting they should have completed the prereading and reading work for chapters 11-13.

Activity #3
Give students the remainder of this class period to get together in their groups to discuss the information they have found about their research projects.

LESSON SEVEN

Objectives
1. To review the main events and ideas from chapters 11-13
2. To preview the study questions for chapters 14-16
3. To familiarize students with the vocabulary in chapters 14-16
4. To read chapters 14-16

Activity #1
Give students a few minutes to formulate answers for the study guide questions for chapters 11-13, and then discuss the answers to the questions in detail. Write the answers on the board or overhead transparency so students can have the correct answers for study purposes.

Activity #2
Give students the remainder of the class period to do the prereading work for chapters 14-16 and to read those chapters silently.

LESSON EIGHT

Objectives
1. To give students the opportunity to practice writing to inform
2. To help students prepare for their group presentations
3. To give the teacher the opportunity to evaluate students' writing skills
4. To review the main events and ideas from chapters 14-16
5. To do the prereading and reading work for chapters 17-18

Activity #1

Give students a few minutes to formulate answers for the study questions for chapters 14-16. (Or, if you prefer, give students a quiz on chapters 14-16 to make sure they have done the assigned reading.) Discuss the answers to the study questions in detail.

Activity #2

Tell students that prior to your next class period they should have done the prereading and reading work for chapters 17-18.

Activity #3

Distribute Writing Assignment #1. Discuss the directions in detail and give students ample time to complete the assignment.

LESSONS NINE AND TEN

<u>Objectives</u>
    1. To broaden students' knowledge of the world in 1650-1700
    2. To evaluate students' understanding of the silent reading assignment
    3. To preview the study questions and vocabulary for chapters 19-21
    4. To read chapters 19-21
    5. To complete the group presentation projects

<u>Activity #1</u>
    Quiz - Distribute quizzes and give students about 10 minutes to complete them.
(Note: The quizzes may either be the short answer study guides or the multiple choice version for chapters 19-21.) Have students exchange papers. Grade the quizzes as a class.

<u>Activity #2</u>
    Tell students that prior to Lesson Eleven they should have done the prereading and reading work for chapters 19-21. (Give students a day/date.)

<u>Activity #3</u>
    Begin the group presentations. The number of class periods devoted to the reports depends on the length of your class period and the abilities of your students. This unit schedules one and a half class periods.

WRITING ASSIGNMENT #1 - *The Witch of Blackbird Pond*

PROMPT
You have been assigned a topic to research for your group. You have done the research and will soon have to give a presentation to the class. As an evaluation of your participation in the group's work, your assignment is to write a composition in which you tell what topic you researched and specifically explain what information you found. This is composition is to be based on your own research, not the research of the entire group.

PREWRITING
Gather together the notes you took as you were researching your topic. Organize them into a logical fashion, making a little outline of your main ideas.

DRAFTING
Write a paragraph in which you introduce the topic you researched.

Write one paragraph for each main idea you found in your research. Fill out each paragraph with details and examples where appropriate.

Write one paragraph (or more if necessary) in which you give a brief evaluation of your sources. Tell which ones were most helpful (and why), which ones were the least helpful (and why), and what you thought of your sources.

Write a concluding paragraph in which you give your personal reactions to the information you found.

PROMPT
When you finish the rough draft of your paper, ask a student who sits near you to read it. After reading your rough draft, he/she should tell you what he/she liked best about your work, which parts were difficult to understand, and ways in which your work could be improved. Reread your paper considering your critic's comments, and make the corrections you think are necessary.

PROOFREADING
Do a final proofreading of your paper double-checking your grammar, spelling, organization, and the clarity of your ideas.

LESSON TEN

Objectives
1. To review the main ideas and events from chapters 19-21
2. To discuss *The Witch of Blackbird Pond* on interpretive and critical levels

Activity #1

Give students time to formulate answers to the study questions for chapters 19-21. Discuss students' answers to the questions.

Activity #2

Choose the questions from the Extra Discussion Questions/Writing Assignments which seem most appropriate for your students. A class discussion of these questions is most effective if students have been given the opportunity to formulate answers to the questions prior to the discussion. To this end, you may either have all the students formulate answers to all the questions, divide your class into groups and assign one or more questions to each group, or you could assign one question to each student in your class. The option you choose will make a difference in the amount of class time needed for this activity.

Activity #3

After students have had ample time to formulate answers to the questions, begin your class discussion of the questions and the ideas presented by the questions. Be sure students take notes during the discussion so they have information to study for the unit test.

EXTRA WRITING ASSIGNMENTS/DISCUSSION QUESTIONS - *The Witch of Blackbird Pond*

Interpretive

1. What are the main conflicts in the story and how are they resolved?

2. In what way is the setting important to the story?

3. From what point(s) of view is the story written.?

4. Where is the climax of the story? Justify your answer.

5. Which events in the novel are "turning points"--events which affect the course of the plot?

6. Is there any humor in the story? If so, where. If not, why not?

7. Make a list of the things Kit did which startled people. Were they out of the ordinary? If so, how? If not, why did these things startle people?

8. Define the word "witch" according to the criteria used in the story. Use examples from the story.

Critical

9. Explain the significance of the title of the book

10. Is the story of *The Witch of Blackbird Pond* believable? Why or why not?

11. Do any of the characters change in the course of the novel? If so, who and how?

12. Are the characters in *The Witch of Blackbird Pond* stereotypes? Explain your answer.

13. Explain the significance of the colors of the bird to which Nat compared Kit, and explain how the bird and Kit were alike.

14. Compare and contrast Mercy, Judith, and Kit.

15. Compare and contrast John, William and Nat.

16. What was Hannah's use as a character in the story?

17. How is the fact that people became ill important to the plot of the story?

The Witch of Blackbird Pond Extra Discussion Questions Page 2

18. Why was it important to the story that John went off to join the militia?

19. What was the purpose of including the parts about the governor and the charter?

20. The time elapsed during the story is about one year. Explain how the seasons relate to the action of the story.

21. Why was Kit disappointed to find out that she had already seen "town"? What was she looking for in a "town"?

22. In what ways did Kit not fit into the Puritan society?

23. Nat's family's home is in Puritan New England. Explain how and why he is different from Matthew Wood and the other Puritans.

24. Compare and contrast the teaching styles of Mercy and Kit.

25. Characterize Elizabeth George Speare's style of writing. How does it contribute to the value of the novel?

Personal Response

26. The witch hunt was a form of persecution. Think of another group of people who are being persecuted today. Who are they and why are they being persecuted?

27. There are many people in the world today who cannot read and write. Suppose someone would come to you and ask you to teach them to read or write. What would you do?

28. Prudence said, "Nobody cares where I go, just so's I get the work done." Do you think Prudence's parents were doing a good job as parents? How much freedom is good, and at what point does too much freedom become a problem? What makes a good parent?

29. Nat asked, "What is treason, Kit?" What is your answer to that question?

30. Would you have liked to have been a part of life in *The Witch of Blackbird Pond*? Why or why not?

31. If you could be any of the characters in the book for a short time, which one would you choose? Why?

32. Did you enjoy reading *The Witch of Blackbird Pond*? Why or why not?

LESSON TWELVE

Objective
   To review all of the vocabulary work done in this unit

Activity
   Choose one (or more) of the vocabulary review activities listed below and spend your class period as directed in the activity. Some of the materials for these review activities are located in the Vocabulary Resource section in this unit.

VOCABULARY REVIEW ACTIVITIES

1. Divide your class into two teams and have an old-fashioned spelling or definition bee.

2. Give each of your students (or students in groups of two, three or four) a *The Witch of Blackbird Pond* Vocabulary Word Search Puzzle. The person (group) to find all of the vocabulary words in the puzzle first wins.

3. Give students a *The Witch of Blackbird Pond* Vocabulary Word Search Puzzle without the word list. The person or group to find the most vocabulary words in the puzzle wins.

4. Use a *The Witch of Blackbird Pond* Vocabulary Crossword Puzzle. Put the puzzle onto a transparency on the overhead projector (so everyone can see it), and do the puzzle together as a class.

5. Give students a *The Witch of Blackbird Pond* Vocabulary Matching Worksheet to do.

6. Divide your class into two teams. Use *The Witch of Blackbird Pond* vocabulary words with their letters jumbled as a word list. Student 1 from Team A faces off against Student 1 from Team B. You write the first jumbled word on the board. The first student (1A or 1B) to unscramble the word wins the chance for his/her team to score points. If 1A wins the jumble, go to student 2A and give him/her a definition. He/she must give you the correct spelling of the vocabulary word which fits that definition. If he/she does, Team A scores a point, and you give student 3A a definition for which you expect a correctly spelled matching vocabulary word. Continue giving Team A definitions until some team member makes an incorrect response. An incorrect response sends the game back to the jumbled-word face off, this time with students 2A and 2B. Instead of repeating giving definitions to the first few students of each team, continue with the student after the one who gave the last incorrect response on the team. For example, if Team B wins the jumbled-word face-off, and student 5B gave the last incorrect answer for Team B, you would start this round of definition questions with student 6B, and so on. The team with the most points wins!

7. Have students write a story in which they correctly use as many vocabulary words as possible. Have students read their compositions orally! Post the most original compositions on your bulletin board!

LESSON THIRTEEN

Objectives
    1. To give students the opportunity to practice writing to express their own opinions/feelings
    2. To give the teacher the opportunity to evaluate students' writing skills

Activity #1

    Distribute Writing Assignment #2. Discuss the directions in detail and give students ample time to complete the assignment.

Activity #2

    While students are doing their group work, call individual students to your desk or some other private area where you can hold a writing conference to discuss students' first writing assignments. A Writing Evaluation Form is included for your convenience.

LESSONS FOURTEEN AND FIFTEEN

Objectives
    1. To give students the opportunity to practice persuasive writing
    2. To follow up on Writing Assignment #2
    3. To give students the opportunity to be creative

Activity #1

    Discuss the travelogue video you showed in the introductory lesson in terms of it's persuasiveness. What things appealed to those who viewed the video? What kinds of things were on the video? (It didn't show pictured of dumps and disgusting alleys; it probably showed beautiful beaches, green and blooming vegetation, etc.) Discuss how the visual and verbal portions of the video worked together to make the place being shown appealing.

NOTE: Also have some travel brochures from various places for students to look at to get ideas about how to make their own brochures.

Activity #2

    Distribute Writing Assignment #3. Discuss the directions in detail and give students ample time to complete the assignment.

    NOTE: This assignment can be done by either individual students or done as a group project if you prefer. If you choose to do it as a group project, the entire group (two or three students) must agree on the place about which the brochure will be written.

WRITING ASSIGNMENT #2 - *The Witch of Blackbird Pond*

PROMPT

Kit sailed from Barbados to New England. Sailing was, in her time, a means of transportation more than a sport for pleasure. Now we think of sailing as something to do on beautiful, sunny summer days with warm breezes. It's refreshing, somewhat romantic, and definitely the material for great daydreams. Close your eyes for a moment and think to yourself, "Ah, if I could sail away . . . ."

Where would you sail to? Your assignment is to finish the sentence, "If I could sail away . . . ." and tell where you would go and what you would do.

PREWRITING

Close your eyes and daydream for a while. Then, write down some ideas about how you would finish your sentence. Jot down notes about where you would go and what you would do.

Describe in detail any scenes in which you can see yourself participating.

DRAFTING

There is no strict format for this assignment. Begin your composition with the sentence you are to finish, finish the sentence, and write several paragraphs about your dream adventure.

PROMPT

Even though there is no strict format for this assignment, it still has to make sense, be written in good English, and communicate your thoughts clearly. When you finish writing your composition, hand it to a friend to read over. After reading your rough draft, he/she should tell you what he/she liked best about your work, which parts were difficult to understand, and ways in which your work could be improved. Reread your paper considering your critic's comments, and make the corrections you think are necessary.

PROOFREADING

Do a final proofreading of your paper double-checking your grammar, spelling, organization, and the clarity of your ideas.

WRITING ASSIGNMENT #3 - *The Witch of Blackbird Pond*

PROMPT

In your last writing assignment, you "sailed away" on an adventure doing some creative writing and expressing your own ideas about things you would like to do. In this assignment, you are to practice persuasive writing by creating a travel brochure (or a video if you would rather make a video) for the place to which you went in your last assignment, persuading people to go to that place.

PREWRITING

Think about travel brochures or videos you have seen in the past. Make a list of the kinds of things that are in the brochures or are shown on the videos you have seen. Now, make a list of those kinds of things for your brochure or video. What things about your place appeal to you? Those same things will probably appeal to other people, too. All these are the things you want to include in your brochure.

Of the things you are going to put into your brochure, which are the most important to get your audience's attention? Make those things the biggest and/or the most obvious things on the brochure. Rank the other things you have on your list according to how important they are to the success of your brochure. Make sure the most important things are included. Use some of the other things if you have space, as fillers.

Make a rough layout of your brochure. Take a sheet of paper, draw boxes where pictures will go (and write in the box what picture will go there), and make other boxes where "copy," written material, will go (and write in the boxes what kind of information will go there).

DRAFTING

Work on your copy first. Write out exactly what will go in your copy boxes. Choose your words carefully. You don't have much space; make every word effective. When you are happy with your copy, make it in a form that will fit in the space you have provided for it on your rough layout.

Find pictures in magazines to cut out and use in your picture boxes. Finding the picture you want in the size you want them is going to be the tricky part. It will take some effort to get what you want.

Put it all together using tacky glue (like sticky notes use so you can pick up and put down several times without wrecking the pictures or copy).

PROMPT

Give the rough draft of your brochure to a classmate to look over. After looking at it, he/she should tell you what he/she liked best about your work, which parts were difficult to understand, and ways in which your work could be improved. Look at your brochure again considering your critic's comments, and make the corrections you think are necessary. Do a final proofreading of your brochure double-checking your grammar, spelling, organization, and the clarity of your ideas.

WRITING EVALUATION FORM - *The Witch of Blackbird Pond*

Name _____ Date _____

Grade _____

Circle One For Each Item:

Grammar: excellent   good   fair   poor

Spelling: excellent   good   fair   poor

Punctuation: excellent   good   fair   poor

Legibility: excellent   good   fair   poor

Strengths:

Weaknesses:

Comments/Suggestions:

LESSON SIXTEEN

Objective

To review the main ideas presented in *The Witch of Blackbird Pond*

Activity #1

Choose one of the review games/activities included in this unit and spend your class period as outlined there. Some materials for these activities are located in the Unit Resource section of this unit.

Activity #2

Remind students that the Unit Test will be in the next class meeting. Stress the review of the Study Guides and their class notes as a last minute, brush-up review for homework.

REVIEW GAMES/ACTIVITIES - *The Witch of Blackbird Pond*

1. Ask the class to make up a unit test for *The Witch of Blackbird Pond*. The test should have 4 sections: matching, true/false, short answer, and essay. Students may use 1/2 period to make the test and then swap papers and use the other 1/2 class period to take a test a classmate has devised. (open book) You may want to use the unit test included in this unit or take questions from the students' unit tests to formulate your own test.

2. Take 1/2 period for students to make up true and false questions (including the answers). Collect the papers and divide the class into two teams. Draw a big tic-tac-toe board on the chalk board. Make one team X and one team O. Ask questions to each side, giving each student one turn. If the question is answered correctly, that students' team's letter (X or O) is placed in the box. If the answer is incorrect, no mark is placed in the box. The object is to get three marks in a row like tic-tac-toe. You may want to keep track of the number of games won for each team.

3. Take 1/2 period for students to make up questions (true/false and short answer). Collect the questions. Divide the class into two teams. You'll alternate asking questions to individual members of teams A & B (like in a spelling bee). The question keeps going from A to B until it is correctly answered, then a new question is asked. A correct answer does not allow the team to get another question. Correct answers are +2 points; incorrect answers are -1 point.

4. Have students pair up and quiz each other from their study guides and class notes.

5. Give students a *The Witch of Blackbird Pond* crossword puzzle to complete.

6. Divide your class into two teams. Use *The Witch of Blackbird Pond* crossword puzzle words with their letters jumbled as a word list. Student 1 from Team A faces off against Student 1 from Team B. You write the first jumbled word on the board. The first student (1A or 1B) to unscramble the word wins the chance for his/her team to score points. If 1A wins the jumble, go to student 2A and give him/her a clue. He/she must give you the correct word which matches that clue. If he/she does, Team A scores a point, and you give student 3A a clue for which you expect another correct response. Continue giving Team A clues until some team member makes an incorrect response. An incorrect response sends the game back to the jumbled-word face off, this time with students 2A and 2B. Instead of repeating giving clues to the first few students of each team, continue with the student after the one who gave the last incorrect response on the team. For example, if Team B wins the jumbled-word face-off, and student 5B gave the last incorrect answer for Team B, you would start this round of clue questions with student 6B, and so on. The team with the most points wins!

UNIT TESTS

SHORT ANSWER UNIT TEST 1 - *The Witch of Blackbird Pond*

I. Matching

___   1. Rachel   A. Kit taught her to read and write

___   2. Prudence   B. Quaker

___   3. Kit   C. The Reverend

___   4. Mercy   D. Lived in Barbados

___   5. John   E. Rich bachelor

___   6. Judith   F. Kit's uncle

___   7. William   G. Studying to be a minister

___   8. Nat   H. Mercy's sister

___   9. Matthew   I. Governor

___   10. Hannah   J. Was crippled by a childhood illness

___   11. The Witch   K. Nat's new ship

___   12. Bulkeley   L. Sailor

___   13. Andros   M. Kit's aunt

Witch of Blackbird Pond Short Answer Unit Test 1 Page 2

II. Short Answer
1. Why did Kit jump off of the long boat?

2. Why did Goodwife Cruff think that Kit was a witch?

3. Why was John surprised that Kit read plays?

4. How did Matthew Wood react to Kit's giving clothes to his daughters?

5. What did Kit think of the church services?

6. Why was the fact that William had started building his house significant?

7. Describe Kit's feelings about the meadows.

Witch of Blackbird Pond Short Answer Unit Test 1 Page 3

8. What did Kit do to anger the schoolmasters?

9. Why didn't Prudence go to school?

10. To what did Nat compare Kit?

11. Why did the people want Hannah?

12. How was Kit proved to be innocent?

The Witch of Blackbird Pond Short Answer Unit Test 1 Page 4

III. Essay

    Think of another title for *The Witch of Blackbird Pond* and explain your choice in detail.

IV. Vocabulary

    Listen to the vocabulary words and write them down. Go back later and write in the correct definitions next to the words.

1.

2.

3.

4.

5.

6.

7.

8.

9.

10.

KEY: SHORT ANSWER UNIT TEST #1 - *The Witch of Blackbird Pond*

I. Matching/Identify

M	1. Rachel	A.	Kit taught her to read and write
A	2. Prudence	B.	Quaker
D	3. Kit	C.	The Reverend
J	4. Mercy	D.	Lived in Barbados
G	5. John	E.	Rich bachelor
H	6. Judith	F.	Kit's uncle
E	7. William	G.	Studying to be a minister
L	8. Nat	H.	Mercy's sister
F	9. Matthew	I.	Governor
B	10. Hannah	J.	Was crippled by a childhood illness
K	11. The Witch	K.	Nat's new ship
C	12. Bulkeley	L.	Sailor
I	13. Andros	M.	Kit's aunt

II. Short Answer

1. Why did Kit jump off of the long boat?
   A little girl had lost her doll in the water, and the captain wouldn't turn around to go get it.
2. Why did Goodwife Cruff think that Kit was a witch?
   Kit could swim. According to the water trials for witches, only witches would stay afloat in water.
3. Why was John surprised that Kit read plays?
   The Puritans believed that the only purpose for reading was to improve one's sinful nature. Reading plays for enjoyment was considered sinful.
4. How did Matthew Wood react to Kit's giving clothes to his daughters?
   He was furious. He demanded that they be returned at once and ordered Kit to clean up her mess.

5. What did Kit think of the church services?

>She detested them. They were long and boring, and she was uncomfortable there.

6. Why was the fact that William had started building his house significant?

>It meant that he had decided to get married; he had chosen his bride.

7. Describe Kit's feelings about the meadows.

>She loved being in the meadows; they were beautiful and made her feel calm and comforted.

8. What did Kit do to anger the schoolmasters?

>She had the children act out a Bible story.

9. Why didn't Prudence go to school?

>Goodwife Cruff said Prudence was too stupid and too big to go to school.

10. To what did Nat compare Kit?

>He compared her to a yellow-green tropical bird with scarlet patches. He said that had the bird been brought to New England, the other birds there would scold and peck at it.

11. Why did the people want Hannah?

>They wanted to kill her because they thought she used a spell to cause the illness which was spreading over the town.

12. How was Kit proved to be innocent?

>Nat brought Prudence to the hearing. She testified that Kit had taught her to read and write, and that she could read Bible stories.

III. Essay: Answers will vary.

IV. Vocabulary

>Choose ten of the vocabulary words to read orally for students to write down.

SHORT ANSWER UNIT TEST 2 - *The Witch of Blackbird Pond*

I. Matching

___   1. Rachel   A. Quaker

___   2. Prudence   B. Mercy's sister

___   3. Kit   C. Lived in Barbados

___   4. Mercy   D. Studying to be a minister

___   5. John   E. Governor

___   6. Judith   F. Rich bachelor

___   7. William   G. The Reverend

___   8. Nat   H. Kit taught her to read and write

___   9. Matthew   I. Kit's uncle

___   10. Hannah   J. Sailor

___   11. The Witch   K. Kit's aunt

___   12. Bulkeley   L. Nat's new ship

___   13. Andros   M. Was crippled by a childhood illness

Witch of Blackbird Pond Short Answer Unit Test 2 Page 2

II. Short Answer

1. How did people on the boat react when Kit said that she could swim? Why?

2. Why was John surprised that Kit read plays?

3. How did Matthew Wood react to Kit's giving clothes to his daughters? Why?

4. Why was the fact that William had started building his house significant?

5. To what did Nat compare Kit?

6. What was Nat's punishment for participating in the Halloween prank?

Witch of Blackbird Pond Short Answer Unit Test 2 Page 3

7. Why did the people want Hannah?

8. What happened to Kit because she was known to be a friend to Hannah?

9. How was Kit proved to be innocent?

10. What change came over Goodman Cruff when he found out that Prudence could read and write?

The Witch of Blackbird Pond Short Answer Unit Test 2 Page 4

III. Composition

Explain the role of religion in *The Witch of Blackbird Pond*.

IV. Vocabulary

Listen to the vocabulary words and spell them. After you have spelled all the words, go back and write down the definitions.

1.

2.

3.

4.

5.

6.

7.

8.

9.

10.

KEY: SHORT ANSWER UNIT TEST 2 *The Witch of Blackbird Pond*

I. Matching (Use this matching key also for the Advanced Short Answer Unit Test)

K	1. Rachel	A.	Quaker
H	2. Prudence	B.	Mercy's sister
C	3. Kit	C.	Lived in Barbados
M	4. Mercy	D.	Studying to be a minister
D	5. John	E.	Governor
B	6. Judith	F.	Rich bachelor
F	7. William	G.	The Reverend
J	8. Nat	H.	Kit taught her to read and write
I	9. Matthew	I.	Kit's uncle
A	10. Hannah	J.	Sailor
L	11. The Witch	K.	Kit's aunt
G	12. Bulkeley	L.	Nat's new ship
E	13. Andros	M.	Was crippled by a childhood illness

II. Short Answer
1. How did people on the boat react when Kit said that she could swim? Why?
    They were surprised and suspicious. Swimming was unnatural, and they thought that only witches could "float."
2. Why was John surprised that Kit read plays?
    The Puritans believed that the only purpose for reading was to improve one's sinful nature. Reading plays for enjoyment was considered sinful.
3. How did Matthew Wood react to Kit's giving clothes to his daughters? Why?
    He was furious. He demanded that they be returned at once and ordered Kit to clean up her mess. Kit's fancy clothes didn't fit with the Puritan belief of wearing plain clothes, nor did it seem appropriate to be giving such lavish gifts.
4. Why was the fact that William had started building his house significant?
    It meant that he had decided to get married; he had chosen his bride.
5. To what did Nat compare Kit?
    He compared her to a yellow-green tropical bird with scarlet patches. He said that had the bird been brought to New England, the other birds there would scold and peck at it.
6. What was Nat's punishment for participating in the Halloween prank?
    He was put into the stocks in the square and was then banished from Wethersfield.
7. Why did the people want Hannah?
    They wanted to kill her because they thought she used a spell to cause the illness which was spreading over the town.
8. What happened to Kit because she was known to be a friend to Hannah?
    She was accused of being a witch and was locked in a shed until her hearing.
9. How was Kit proved to be innocent?
    Nat brought Prudence to the hearing. She testified that Kit had taught her to read and write, and that she could read Bible stories.
10. What change came over Goodman Cruff when he found out that Prudence could read and write?
    He was very proud of Prudence. He became very brave and stood up to his wife. Goodman Cruff withdrew the charges against Kit.

III. Composition: Answers will vary.

IV. Vocabulary: Choose ten vocabulary words to dictate to your students for this section.

ADVANCED SHORT ANSWER UNIT TEST - *The Witch of Blackbird Pond*

I. Matching

___   1. Rachel   A. Quaker

___   2. Prudence   B. Mercy's sister

___   3. Kit   C. Lived in Barbados

___   4. Mercy   D. Studying to be a minister

___   5. John   E. Governor

___   6. Judith   F. Rich bachelor

___   7. William   G. The Reverend

___   8. Nat   H. Kit taught her to read and write

___   9. Matthew   I. Kit's uncle

___   10. Hannah   J. Sailor

___   11. The Witch   K. Kit's aunt

___   12. Bulkeley   L. Nat's new ship

___   13. Andros   M. Was crippled by a childhood illness

Witch of Blackbird Pond Advanced Short Answer Unit Test Page 2

II. Short Answer

1. Make a list of the things Kit did which startled people. Were they out of the ordinary? If so, how? If not, why did these things startle people?

2. Explain the significance of the colors of the bird to which Nat compared Kit, and explain how the bird and Kit were alike.

3. Compare and contrast Mercy, Judith, and Kit.

4. Compare and contrast John, William and Nat.

Witch of Blackbird Pond Advanced Short Answer Unit Test Page 3

5. What was Hannah's use as a character in the story?

6. How is the fact that people became ill important to the plot of the story?

7. Why was Kit disappointed to find out that she had already seen "town"? What was she looking for in a "town"?

8. In what ways did Kit not fit into the Puritan society?

Witch of Blackbird Pond Advanced Short Answer Unit Test Page 4

III. Composition

The *Washington Post* called *The Witch of Blackbird Pond*, "A spellbinding novel of suspense and romance. . . ." Defend that statement using your knowledge of the novel.

The Witch of Blackbird Pond Advanced Short Answer Unit Test Page 5

IV. Vocabulary

    Listen to the vocabulary words and write them down. After you have written down all the words, write a paragraph using all of the vocabulary words. The paragraph must in some way relate to *The Witch of Blackbird Pond*.

MULTIPLE CHOICE UNIT TEST 1 - *The Witch of Blackbird Pond*

I. Matching

___ 1. Rachel   A. Kit taught her to read and write

___ 2. Prudence   B. Quaker

___ 3. Kit   C. The Reverend

___ 4. Mercy   D. Lived in Barbados

___ 5. John   E. Rich bachelor

___ 6. Judith   F. Kit's uncle

___ 7. William   G. Studying to be a minister

___ 8. Nat   H. Mercy's sister

___ 9. Matthew   I. Governor

___ 10. Hannah   J. Was crippled by a childhood illness

___ 11. The Witch   K. Nat's new ship

___ 12. Bulkeley   L. Sailor

___ 13. Andros   M. Kit's aunt

Witch of Blackbird Pond Multiple Choice Unit Test 1 Page 2

II. Multiple Choice

1. Why had Kit lived with her grandfather?
    a. Her parents could not afford to keep her, and they sent her to live with him.
    b. Her parents were killed when she was very young. He was her nearest relative.
    c. Her parents were missionaries. They left her with him when they went to India, but they had never returned.
    d. He was old and needed company and someone to take care of him. He paid Kit's parents a large sum of money for the assistance.

2. What about Kit's reading surprised John?
    a. He was surprised that she could read at all, because none of the other women he knew could read.
    b. She owned her own collection of books, and he had never met anyone before who owned more than a Bible.
    c. She was reading plays, which was considered sinful.
    d. She was able to read Latin and Greek as well as English.

3. Why weren't Kit's relatives at the dock to meet her?
    a. They believed it was a waste of time to leave their work when she could find her own way to their house.
    b. They had been told the wrong day of arrival for the ship. They thought it was coming the following week.
    c. They were all sick and were not able to leave their houses.
    d. They didn't know she was coming.

4. True or False: Rachel is a loving, caring, truly good woman. She tends to those who are less fortunate and tries to carry out her duties as a Puritan woman in the best way she knows how.
    a. True
    b. False

5. What was wrong with Mercy?
    a. She had been born prematurely and had not developed correctly.
    b. She had been struck by lightning.
    c. She had been crippled by a childhood disease.
    d. She had fallen off of a roof and there was no doctor to set her leg, so it had healed incorrectly.

Witch of Blackbird Pond Multiple Choice Unit Test 1 Page 3

6. What did Kit think of the church services?
    a. She detested them. She thought they were long and boring.
    b. She enjoyed the solemnity and ritual.
    c. She didn't care about them one way or another.
    d. She thought the religious people of the village were hypocrites and wished they would follow the things they were taught in the church services.

7. Why did Dr. Bulkeley think Matthew was a traitor?
    a. He believed in slavery.
    b. He thought all men should be allowed to worship as they pleased.
    c. He did not like the King's appointed governor.
    d. He thought the colonies should be free from rule by England.

8. How did Kit feel about the meadows?
    a. She loved being there; they were beautiful and made her feel calm and comforted.
    b. She didn't like them. The grasses made her sneeze and itch.
    TWO CHOICES ONLY

9. What did Kit do to anger the schoolmasters?
    a. She read poetry to the children.
    b. She taught them to draw pictures of happy things.
    c. She had them act out a Bible story.
    d. She allowed the children to have recess.

10. Why did Kit go to see Mr. Kimberly?
    a. She went to demand her pay.
    b. She went to apologize and try to get her job back.
    c. She went to recommend Mercy for the position.
    d. She went to tell him exactly what she thought of him.

11. Why didn't Prudence go to school?
    a. She was needed at home to care for the younger children.
    b. Her mother said she was too stupid and too big to go to school.
    c. Her father didn't think book learning was important for a girl.
    d. She was afraid to leave her home and interact with other children.

Witch of Blackbird Pond Multiple Choice Unit Test 1 Page 4

12. What did Nat and Kit do for Hannah?
    a. They cut firewood and made a new roof for her house.
    b. They harvested the vegetables from her garden.
    c. They built a new room onto her house.
    d. They took her shopping in town.

13. Why was the charter safe?
    a. The King had the original copy.
    b. The governor had committed it to memory.
    c. The minister was keeping it.
    d. It had been taken away from the governor.

14. Where did John go?
    a. He went to Boston to study at the Harvard School of Divinity.
    b. He went off to join the militia to fight.
    c. He went to become a missionary in India.
    d. He went to live in a neighboring town.

15. Where did Kit hide Hannah?
    a. She hid her in the Wood's barn.
    b. She hid her in the Dolphin.
    c. She hid her in her own attic.
    d. She hid her in a closet at the church.

16. True or False: The people wanted Hannah because they thought she knew a remedy for the illness.
    a. True
    b. False

17. How did the townspeople suppose Hannah had escaped?
    a. They thought she had changed herself into a fish and had escaped by the river.
    b. They thought she had changed herself into a bird and had flown away.
    c. They thought she had made herself invisible and was still among them.
    d. They thought she had changed herself into a mouse and had run away.

18. True or False: Kit was also accused of being a witch because she was known to be a friend of Hannah.
    a. True
    b. False

Witch of Blackbird Pond Multiple Choice Unit Test 1 Page 5

19. What evidence did Goodman Cruff Bring forth at the hearing?
    a. He said he had heard Prudence talking about casting spells she had learned from Kate.
    b. He showed the people a gold coin that Kit had given to Prudence.
    c. He brought a small bundle of things that Prudence had tied in a handkerchief. The bundle contained a lock of hair, a bird's feather, some grass, and two pebbles. He thought they were evil talismans.
    d. He produced the little copy book in which Prudence had copied her name.

20. True or False: Kit was proven innocent by Prudence's testimony and demonstration of her reading and writing abilities.
    a. True
    b. False

21. True or False: William had stayed away during Kit's arrest and trial because he had been ill.
    a. True
    b. False

22. Who was going to be married?
    a. Kit and William were going to be married, as were Mercy and John.
    b. Judith and William were going to be married, as were Kit and John.
    c. Judith and William were going to be married, as were Mercy and John.
    d. Kit and Nat were going to be married, as were Mercy and William.

23. How was Kit going to afford passage back to Barbados?
    a. Matthew Wood gave her the money, and she said she would repay it after she arrived back in Barbados.
    b. Nat gave her the money.
    c. She was going to teach for a few months and use the salary for passage.
    d. She was going to sell her beautiful clothes.

24. What did Kit realize?
    a. She realized that she wanted to convert to the Quaker way of life.
    b. She realized that she loved Nat, and he loved her.
    c. She realized she was very angry for the way the people in Wethersfield had treated her.
    d. She realized that she had no feelings at all for her relatives.

Witch of Blackbird Pond Multiple Choice Unit Test 1 Page 6

III. Composition

1. Compare and contrast Mercy, Judith and Kit.

2. Compare and contrast John, William, and Nat.

The Witch of Blackbird Pond Multiple Choice Unit Test 1 Page 7

IV. Vocabulary: Multiple choice. Write in the letter of the definition that matches the word.

____	1. DOCILE		A. A patronizing manner or behavior
____	2. CRONIES		B. Characterized by reason, sanity or self-control
____	3. PUNCTILIOUS		C. Emotionally touching or moving; pungent smell or taste
____	4. WISTFULLY		D. State of being vexed, irritated, or annoyed
____	5. POIGNANT		E. Teasingly
____	6. CHAGRIN		F. Old friends; close companions
____	7. INFIDEL		G. Easy to manage or discipline
____	8. NONCHALANCE		H. Very careful about every detail of behavior
____	9. PROVOCATIVELY		I. Showing cool lack of concern
____	10. CONDESCENSION		J. The property a woman brings to her husband at marriage
____	11. EXASPERATION		K. Longing pensively; expressing vague yearnings
____	12. DOWRIES		L. Made afraid; made timid; cowed
____	13. SURREPTITIOUSLY		M. In a secret, stealthy way; clandestine
____	14. ANGUISH		N. Mortification; embarrassment
____	15. INTIMIDATED		O. Great suffering as from worry, grief or pain
____	16. RESOLUTELY		P. Showing a fixed, firm purpose; determined
____	17. BLASPHEMY		Q. One who does not believe in a particular religion
____	18. TANTALIZINGLY		R. Cleverness, originality, skill
____	19. SOBERED		S. Tending to provoke as to action, thought or feeling
____	20. INGENUITY		T. Contemptuous speech or action against God

MULTIPLE CHOICE UNIT TEST 2 - *The Witch of Blackbird Pond*

I. Matching

___ 1. Rachel   A. Quaker

___ 2. Prudence   B. Mercy's sister

___ 3. Kit   C. Lived in Barbados

___ 4. Mercy   D. Studying to be a minister

___ 5. John   E. Governor

___ 6. Judith   F. Rich bachelor

___ 7. William   G. The Reverend

___ 8. Nat   H. Kit taught her to read and write

___ 9. Matthew   I. Kit's uncle

___ 10. Hannah   J. Sailor

___ 11. The Witch   K. Kit's aunt

___ 12. Bulkeley   L. Nat's new ship

___ 13. Andros   M. Was crippled by a childhood illness

Witch of Blackbird Pond Multiple Choice Unit Test 2 Page 2

II. Multiple Choice

1. Why had Kit lived with her grandfather?
    a. He was old and needed company and someone to take care of him. He paid Kit's parents a large sum of money for the assistance.
    b. Her parents could not afford to keep her, and they sent her to live with him.
    c. Her parents were killed when she was very young. He was her nearest relative.
    d. Her parents were missionaries. They left her with him when they went to India, but they had never returned.

2. What about Kit's reading surprised John?
    a. She was able to read Latin and Greek as well as English.
    b. She owned her own collection of books, and he had never met anyone before who owned more than a Bible.
    c. He was surprised that she could read at all, because none of the other women he knew could read.
    d. She was reading plays, which was considered sinful.

3. Why weren't Kit's relatives at the dock to meet her?
    a. They didn't know she was coming.
    b. They had been told the wrong day of arrival for the ship. They thought it was coming the following week.
    c. They believed it was a waste of time to leave their work when she could find her own way to their house.
    d. They were all sick and were not able to leave their houses.

4. True of False: Rachel is a loving, caring, truly good woman. She tends to those who are less fortunate and tries to carry out her duties as a Puritan woman in the best way she knows how.
    a. True
    b. False

5. What was wrong with Mercy?
    a. She had been struck by lightning.
    b. She had been crippled by a childhood disease.
    c. She had been born prematurely and had not developed correctly.
    d. She had fallen off of a roof and there was no doctor to set her leg, so it had healed incorrectly.

Witch of Blackbird Pond Multiple Choice Unit Test 2 Page 3

6. What did Kit think of the church services?
    a. She thought the religious people of the village were hypocrites and wished they would follow the things they were taught in the church services.
    b. She enjoyed the solemnity and ritual.
    c. She detested them. She thought they were long and boring.
    d. She didn't care about them one way or another.

7. Why did Dr. Bulkeley think Matthew was a traitor?
    a. He did not like the King's appointed governor.
    b. He believed in slavery.
    c. He thought all men should be allowed to worship as they pleased.
    d. He thought the colonies should be free from rule by England.

8. How did Kit feel about the meadows?
    a. She didn't like them; she much preferred to sit indoors and read a book.
    b. She loved being there; they were beautiful and made her feel calm and comforted.
    TWO CHOICES ONLY

9. What did Kit do to anger the schoolmasters?
    a. She allowed the children to have recess.
    b. She read poetry to the children.
    c. She taught them to draw pictures of happy things.
    d. She had them act out a Bible story.

10. Why did Kit go to see Mr. Kimberly?
    a. She went to recommend Mercy for the position.
    b. She went to demand her pay.
    c. She went to apologize and try to get her job back.
    d. She went to tell him exactly what she thought of him.

11. Why didn't Prudence go to school?
    a. Her mother said she was too stupid and too big to go to school.
    b. She was needed at home to care for the younger children.
    c. Her father didn't think book learning was important for a girl.
    d. She was afraid to leave her home and interact with other children.

Witch of Blackbird Pond Multiple Choice Unit Test 2 Page 4

12. What did Nat and Kit do for Hannah?
    a. They took her shopping in town.
    b. They cut firewood and made a new roof for her house.
    c. They built a new room onto her house.
    d. They harvested the vegetables from her garden.

13. Why was the charter safe?
    a. The minister was keeping it.
    b. The governor had committed it to memory.
    c. It had been taken away from the governor.
    d. The King had the original copy.

14. Where did John go?
    a. He went to Boston to study at the Harvard School of Divinity.
    b. He went to become a missionary in India.
    c. He went off to join the militia to fight.
    d. He went to live in a neighboring town.

15. Where did Kit hide Hannah?
    a. She hid her in a closet at the church.
    b. She hid her in the Wood's barn.
    c. She hid her in her own attic.
    d. She hid her in *The Dolphin*.

16. True or False: The people wanted Hannah because they thought she was responsible for the illness.
    a. True
    b. False

17. How did the townspeople suppose Hannah had escaped?
    a. They thought she had changed herself into a fish and had escaped by the river.
    b. They thought she had changed herself into a mouse and had run away.
    c. They thought she had made herself invisible and was still among them.
    d. None of the above.

18. True or False: Kit was also accused of being a witch because she was known to be a friend of Hannah.
    a. True
    b. False

Witch of Blackbird Pond Multiple Choice Unit Test 2 Page 5

19. What evidence did Goodman Cruff Bring forth at the hearing?
    a. He said he had heard Prudence talking about casting spells she had learned from Kate.
    b. He showed the people a gold coin that Kit had given to Prudence.
    c. He produced the little copy book in which Prudence had copied her name.
    d. He brought a small bundle of things that Prudence had tied in a handkerchief. The bundle contained a lock of hair, a bird's feather, some grass, and two pebbles. He thought they were evil talismans.

20. True or False: Kit was proven guilty by Prudence's testimony and demonstration of her reading and writing abilities.
    a. True
    b. False

21. True or False: William had stayed away during Kit's arrest and trial because he had been ill.
    a. True
    b. False

22. Who was going to be married?
    a. Judith and William were going to be married, as were Kit and John.
    b. Kit and Nat were going to be married, as were Mercy and William.
    c. Kit and William were going to be married, as were Mercy and John.
    d. Judith and William were going to be married, as were Mercy and John.

23. How was Kit going to afford passage back to Barbados?
    a. She was going to sell her beautiful clothes.
    b. Nat gave her the money.
    c. She was going to teach for a few months and use the salary for passage.
    d. Matthew Wood gave her the money, and she said she would repay it after she arrived back in Barbados.

24. What did Kit realize?
    a. She realized that she wanted to convert to the Quaker way of life.
    b. She realized that she had no feelings at all for her relatives.
    c. She realized that she loved Nat, and he loved her.
    d. She realized she was very angry for the way the people in Wethersfield had treated her.

The Witch of Blackbird Pond Multiple Choice Unit Test 2 Page 6

III. Composition

1. Explain the significance of the colors of the bird to which Nat compared Kit, and explain how Kit and the bird were alike.

2. In what ways did Kit not fit into Puritan society?

3. What was Hannah's use as a character in the story?

Witch of Blackbird Pond Multiple Choice Unit Test 2 Page 7

IV. Vocabulary Match the correct definitions to the words.

_____ 1. INGENUITY   A. The property a woman brings to her husband at marriage

_____ 2. CUFF   B. Ridicule; false, derisive or impertinent imitation

_____ 3. REPROOF   C. Maintained

_____ 4. SUSTAINED   D. One who does not believe in a particular religion

_____ 5. SOBERED   E. Feeling or showing regret

_____ 6. PIOUS   F. Showing a gay, cheerful disposition; carefree

_____ 7. INCREDULOUS   G. Seemingly virtuous; showing religious devotion

_____ 8. EXHILARATING   H. Gradually, slightly, so as to be difficult to perceive

_____ 9. RUEFULLY   I. Characterized by reason, sanity or self-control

_____ 10. IMPERCEPTIBLY   J. Great fear or shock that makes one feel helpless

_____ 11. RESOLUTELY   K. Rebuke; censure; find fault with

_____ 12. ANGUISH   L. Showing a fixed, firm purpose; determined

_____ 13. INFIDEL   M. Cleverness, originality, skill

_____ 14. BLITHELY   N. Invigorating or stimulating

_____ 15. QUALMS   O. Feelings of uneasiness or doubt

_____ 16. MOCKERY   P. Difficult to do

_____ 17. CONSTERNATION   Q. Doubting; skeptical; unwilling or unable to believe

_____ 18. REFUGE   R. To strike with open hand; a slap or blow

_____ 19. ARDUOUS   S. A place of safety

_____ 20. DOWRIES   T. Great suffering as from worry, grief or pain

ANSWER SHEET - *The Witch of Blackbird Pond*
Multiple Choice Unit Tests

I. Matching	II. Multiple Choice	IV. Vocabulary
1. ___	1. ___	1. ___
2. ___	2. ___	2. ___
3. ___	3. ___	3. ___
4. ___	4. ___	4. ___
5. ___	5. ___	5. ___
6. ___	6. ___	6. ___
7. ___	7. ___	7. ___
8. ___	8. ___	8. ___
9. ___	9. ___	9. ___
10. ___	10. ___	10. ___
11. ___	11. ___	11. ___
12. ___	12. ___	12. ___
13. ___	13. ___	13. ___
	14. ___	14. ___
	15. ___	15. ___
	16. ___	16. ___
	17. ___	17. ___
	18. ___	18. ___
	19. ___	19. ___
	20. ___	20. ___
	21. ___	
	22. ___	
	23. ___	
	24. ___	

ANSWER KEY - *The Witch of Blackbird Pond*
Multiple Choice Unit Tests

Answers to Unit Test 1 are in the left column. Answers to Unit Test 2 are in the right column.

I. Matching	II. Multiple Choice	IV. Vocabulary
1. M K	1. B C	1. G M
2. A H	2. C D	2. F R
3. D C	3. D A	3. H K
4. J M	4. A A	4. K C
5. G D	5. C B	5. C I
6. H B	6. A C	6. N G
7. E F	7. C A	7. Q Q
8. L J	8. A B	8. I N
9. F I	9. C D	9. S E
10. B A	10. B C	10. A H
11. K L	11. B A	11. D L
12. C G	12. A B	12. J T
13. I E	13. D C	13. M D
	14. B C	14. O F
	15. B D	15. L O
	16. B A	16. P B
	17. D B	17. T J
	18. A A	18. E S
	19. D C	19. B P
	20. A B	20. R A
	21. B B	
	22. C D	
	23. D A	
	24. B C	

UNIT RESOURCE MATERIALS

BULLETIN BOARD IDEAS - *The Witch of Blackbird Pond*

1. Save one corner of the board for the best of students' *The Witch of Blackbird Pond* writing assignments.

2. Take one of the word search puzzles from the extra activities section and with a marker copy it over in a large size on the bulletin board. Write the clue words to find to one side. Invite students prior to and after class to find the words and circle them on the bulletin board.

3. Title the board *The Witch of Blackbird Pond*: A NOVEL FULL OF CHARACTERS. Find pictures in magazines (or perhaps your library has a file of pictures) of people who look like the various characters in the novel. Place the picture on colorful paper, write the character's name under the picture (or next to it) and write a brief description of the character by it. You may wish to arrange these pictures on a genealogical table to show the relationships among the characters.

4. Write several of the most significant quotations from the book onto the board on brightly colored paper.

5. Make a bulletin board listing the vocabulary words for this unit. As you complete sections of the novel and discuss the vocabulary for each section, write the definitions on the bulletin board. (If your board is one students face frequently, it will help them learn the words.)

6. Post a map of the world on which you locate Barbados and other places mentioned in the novel.

7. Look in your library's picture file to find pictures of life in Puritan New England in the late 1600's. Make half of your bulletin board about Puritan New England and the other half showing pictures of Barbados (or other similar Caribbean islands).

8. Make a bulletin board about Quakers.

9. Make a bulletin board about community life; ways in which different neighborhoods or communities are different (and/or how they are alike).

10. Make a bulletin board about careers related to the story: teaching, shipping, the ministry, medicine, etc.

EXTRA ACTIVITIES - *Witch of Blackbird Pond*

One of the difficulties in teaching a novel is that all students don't read at the same speed. One student who likes to read may take the book home and finish it in a day or two. Sometimes a few students finish the in-class assignments early. The problem, then, is finding suitable extra activities for students.

One thing you can do is to keep a little library in the classroom. For this unit on *The Witch of Blackbird Pond*, biographical information about Elizabeth George Speare would be interesting for some students. You can include other related books and articles about the Salem witch trials of 1692, witchcraft, the supernatural, shipping industry, related careers (teaching, shipping, medicine, etc.), or critics' articles about *The Witch of Blackbird Pond*.

Other things you may keep on hand are puzzles. We have made some relating directly to *The Witch of Blackbird Pond* for you. Feel free to duplicate them.

Some students may like to draw. You might devise a contest or allow some extra-credit grade for students who draw characters or scenes from *The Witch of Blackbird Pond*. Note, too, that if the students do not want to keep their drawings you may pick up some extra bulletin board materials this way. If you have a contest and you supply the prize (a CD or something like that perhaps), you could, possibly, make the drawing itself a non-refundable entry fee.

The pages which follow contain games, puzzles and worksheets. The keys, when appropriate, immediately follow the puzzle or worksheet. There are two main groups of activities: one group for the unit; that is, generally relating to *The Witch of Blackbird Pond* text, and another group of activities related strictly to *The Witch of Blackbird Pond* vocabulary.

Directions for these games, puzzles and worksheets are self-explanatory. The object here is to provide you with extra materials you may use in any way you choose.

MORE ACTIVITIES - *The Witch of Blackbird Pond*

1. Pick a chapter or scene with a great deal of dialogue and have the students act it out on a stage. (Perhaps you could assign various scenes to different groups of students so more than one scene could be acted and more students could participate.)

2. Use some of the related topics (noted earlier for an in-class library) as topics for research, reports or written papers, or as topics for guest speakers.

3. Take short scenes from the novel. Assign parts in the scenes to various students (so that each student has a part). Students should memorize their lines and dress up as their characters to perform their scenes in front of the class in your classroom or on stage.

4. Have students design a book cover (front and back and inside flaps) for *The Witch of Blackbird Pond*.

5. Have students design a bulletin board (ready to be put up; not just sketched) for *The Witch of Blackbird Pond*.

7. Discuss the psychological impact of moving from place to place and ways to deal with the feelings that moving from place to place creates.

8. Have students pretend they have to move (at least 1000 miles away) and make all the necessary plans for a successful move. (This could also be a group activity.)

9. Take a day to discuss life at a harbor. What goes on there? Compare and contrast the importance of shipping in the late 1700's with the importance of shipping today.

10. Take a field trip to see how our courts work. Sit in on a criminal jury trial at your courthouse.

11. Discuss how the Puritan work ethic has embedded itself into our culture and the ways in which it is evident today.

WORD SEARCH - *The Witch of Blackbird Pond*

All words in this list are associated with *The Witch of Blackbird Pond*. The words are placed backwards, forward, diagonally, up and down. The included words are listed below the word searches.

```
C G B W C G Z K K H J B Q P M Y N T N N
R L P W I W K F T S N J I L V E J H P B
G W O X X L Q D H R S D K R P U R C G W
W R I T E W L S Y A L P R U D E N C E B
K E I T H E H I O Z N Z E I W F S H Y Y
Z K T C A E C X A R S N T A L T T F L L
N A T H D E S U O M D H A D R T J O H N
C I C Y E R T O V F S N O H A E A C F R
W A T M E R I Q D M F L A M B H R O P H
R R V W P L S B J A P U B L R U B Y B C
K X O X V R E F K H B F R R H P Q J K P
D L C T E Y J K I C H R N C L V F O K L
F G G K I Y G N L E A D A T M Q O M S M
Q B A Q Z A V X Z U L L J B S R S S H B
T U J K M Y R R Q C B D B R B R H M V C
Q B N Q C H Z T M Q K Y D Y X R L V M B
I L L U M I N A T E D B A P P Z N Z C M
W R T Z W S V P P Y J S H K Y S W N D C
```

ANDROS	CRUFF	MATTHEW	SAYBROOK
BARBADOS	DOLPHIN	MERCY	SHED
BIRD	FLOWERS	MOUSE	SPEARE
BLACKBIRD	HANNAH	NAT	TRAITOR
BOAT	ILLUMINATED	PLAYS	WETHERSFIELD
BULKELEY	JOHN	PRUDENCE	WILLIAM
CHURCH	JUDITH	QUAKER	WITCH
CLOTHES	KIT	RACHAEL	WRITE

KEY: WORD SEARCH - *The Witch of Blackbird Pond*

All words in this list are associated with *The Witch of Blackbird Pond*. The words are placed backwards, forward, diagonally, up and down. The included words are listed below the word searches.

```
                C     W                       B        M
                 L     I                       I        E  J
                  O     L     H     S           R        U   R           W
             W R I T E     L S Y A L P R U D E N C E
              E I     H E H I O     N   E I           H Y
              K T C A E         A R   N T A         T
           N A T H D E S U O M D H A D R T J O H N
              I C Y E R     O   F   N O H A E A C
            W A     E R I     D       F L A M     R O
            R R   W     L S B   A P U         U     B
                  O     R E F K H B   R   H         K
                L   T E     K I C   R   C       O
             F   K I     N L E A   A           O
                  A     A         U L L   B   R
               U         R         B D B   B
             Q                     T           Y
             I L L U M I N A T E D   A
                                     S
```

ANDROS	CRUFF	MATTHEW	SAYBROOK
BARBADOS	DOLPHIN	MERCY	SHED
BIRD	FLOWERS	MOUSE	SPEARE
BLACKBIRD	HANNAH	NAT	TRAITOR
BOAT	ILLUMINATED	PLAYS	WETHERSFIELD
BULKELEY	JOHN	PRUDENCE	WILLIAM
CHURCH	JUDITH	QUAKER	WITCH
CLOTHES	KIT	RACHAEL	WRITE

CROSSWORD - *The Witch of Blackbird Pond*

CROSSWORD CLUES - *The Witch of Blackbird Pond*

ACROSS
1. The Reverend
4. Mercy's sister
6. Kit's uncle
10. Myself
11. A group of men ___ William's new home on Halloween
17. Kit's aunt
19. Suffer from lack of food
20. Take action
21. Belonging to me
22. Buzzing insect
23. Distress signal
25. Goodwife ___; somber mother of Prudence
27. Kit tried to give these to the Woods, but Matthew wouldn't allow it
31. Nat compared Kit to a tropical ___
33. Place where a boat ties up
34. Two thousand pounds
35. Shout
38. Hannah Tupper's religion
39. Goodwife Cruff thought Kit was a ___ because she didn't drown
40. Mistress Eaton spent her summers there
42. Kit was locked in a ___ until her hearing
43. Ceremony in which people get married
44. Author's main ideas throughout a book

DOWN
2. Came from Barbados
3. Sight organ
4. Studying to be a minister
5. Pronoun for belonging to Nat
6. Was crippled by a childhood illness
7. Rich bachelor
8. The Witch of ___ Pond
9. Kit met John Holbrook on the boat to ___
12. The townspeople thought Hannah had changed herself into a ___
13. Governor
14. Kit taught her to read and write
15. Sailor
16. Reading these for enjoyment was considered sinful
18. Kit's former home
24. Kit jumped off the long ___ to get a doll
26. Prudence left ___ for Kit
28. Quaker woman
29. Author
30. Kit looked up and saw it while lying on her back in the meadow
32. Kit detested going to ___ services
36. Make able to
37. Kit taught Prudence to read and ___
41. A single

CROSSWORD ANSWER KEY - *The Witch of Blackbird Pond*

MATCHING QUIZ/WORKSHEET 1 - *The Witch of Blackbird Pond*

____	1. HANNAH	A. Kit met John Holbrook on the boat to ____
____	2. WETHERSFIELD	B. Kit jumped off the long ____ to get a doll
____	3. WITCH	C. Mercy's sister
____	4. BOAT	D. The townspeople thought Hannah had changed herself into a ____
____	5. JOHN	E. Came from Barbados
____	6. RACHAEL	F. Hannah Tupper's religion
____	7. JUDITH	G. The Witch of ____ Pond
____	8. NAT	H. Kit's aunt
____	9. MOUSE	I. Studying to be a minister
____	10. WILLIAM	J. Mistress Eaton spent her summers there
____	11. TRAITOR	K. Kit taught Prudence to read and ____
____	12. WRITE	L. Sailor
____	13. SAYBROOK	M. A group of men ____ William's new home on Halloween
____	14. ANDROS	N. Rich bachelor
____	15. CHURCH	O. Dr. Bulkeley thought Matthew was a ____
____	16. BLACKBIRD	P. Goodwife Cruff thought Kit was a ____ because she didn't drown
____	17. ILLUMINATED	Q. Kit detested going to ____ services
____	18. QUAKER	R. Author
____	19. KIT	S. Governor
____	20. SPEARE	T. Quaker woman

KEY: MATCHING QUIZ/WORKSHEET 1 - *The Witch of Blackbird Pond*

_T_	1. HANNAH	A. Kit met John Holbrook on the boat to ___
_A_	2. WETHERSFIELD	B. Kit jumped off the long ___ to get a doll
_P_	3. WITCH	C. Mercy's sister
_B_	4. BOAT	D. The townspeople thought Hannah had changed herself into a ___
_I_	5. JOHN	E. Came from Barbados
_H_	6. RACHAEL	F. Hannah Tupper's religion
_C_	7. JUDITH	G. The Witch of ____ Pond
_L_	8. NAT	H. Kit's aunt
_D_	9. MOUSE	I. Studying to be a minister
_N_	10. WILLIAM	J. Mistress Eaton spent her summers there
_O_	11. TRAITOR	K. Kit taught Prudence to read and ___
_K_	12. WRITE	L. Sailor
_J_	13. SAYBROOK	M. A group of men ___ William's new home on Halloween
_S_	14. ANDROS	N. Rich bachelor
_Q_	15. CHURCH	O. Dr. Bulkeley thought Matthew was a ___
_G_	16. BLACKBIRD	P. Goodwife Cruff thought Kit was a ___ because she didn't drown
_M_	17. ILLUMINATED	Q. Kit detested going to ___ services
_F_	18. QUAKER	R. Author
_E_	19. KIT	S. Governor
_R_	20. SPEARE	T. Quaker woman

MATCHING QUIZ/WORKSHEET 2 - *The Witch of Blackbird Pond*

____	1. WILLIAM	A. Nat compared Kit to a tropical ___
____	2. ILLUMINATED	B. Kit taught Prudence to read and ___
____	3. WRITE	C. Rich bachelor
____	4. TRAITOR	D. Mistress Eaton spent her summers there
____	5. CRUFF	E. Sailor
____	6. SPEARE	F. Kit met John Holbrook on the boat to ___
____	7. CLOTHES	G. The Reverend
____	8. SAYBROOK	H. Dr. Bulkeley thought Matthew was a ___
____	9. BIRD	I. Goodwife ___; somber mother of Prudence
____	10. FLOWERS	J. Boat where Kit hid Hannah
____	11. BULKELEY	K. Goodwife Cruff thought Kit was a ___ because she didn't drown
____	12. MATTHEW	L. Kit tried to give these to the Woods, but Matthew wouldn't allow it
____	13. BARBADOS	M. Kit's uncle
____	14. HANNAH	N. Kit's former home
____	15. NAT	O. A group of men ___ William's new home on Halloween
____	16. DOLPHIN	P. Author
____	17. MOUSE	Q. Prudence left ___ for Kit
____	18. WETHERSFIELD	R. Quaker woman
____	19. CHURCH	S. The townspeople thought Hannah had changed herself into a ___
____	20. WITCH	T. Kit detested going to ___ services

KEY: MATCHING QUIZ/WORKSHEET 2 - *The Witch of Blackbird Pond*

_C_   1. WILLIAM   A. Nat compared Kit to a tropical ___

_O_   2. ILLUMINATED   B. Kit taught Prudence to read and ___

_B_   3. WRITE   C. Rich bachelor

_H_   4. TRAITOR   D. Mistress Eaton spent her summers there

_I_   5. CRUFF   E. Sailor

_P_   6. SPEARE   F. Kit met John Holbrook on the boat to ___

_L_   7. CLOTHES   G. The Reverend

_D_   8. SAYBROOK   H. Dr. Bulkeley thought Matthew was a ___

_A_   9. BIRD   I. Goodwife ___; somber mother of Prudence

_Q_   10. FLOWERS   J. Boat where Kit hid Hannah

_G_   11. BULKELEY   K. Goodwife Cruff thought Kit was a ___ because she didn't drown

_M_   12. MATTHEW   L. Kit tried to give these to the Woods, but Matthew wouldn't allow it

_N_   13. BARBADOS   M. Kit's uncle

_R_   14. HANNAH   N. Kit's former home

_E_   15. NAT   O. A group of men ___ William's new home on Halloween

_J_   16. DOLPHIN   P. Author

_S_   17. MOUSE   Q. Prudence left ___ for Kit

_F_   18. WETHERSFIELD   R. Quaker woman

_T_   19. CHURCH   S. The townspeople thought Hannah had changed herself into a ___

_K_   20. WITCH   T. Kit detested going to ___ services

JUGGLE LETTER REVIEW GAME CLUE SHEET - *The Witch of Blackbird Pond*

SCRAMBLED	WORD	CLUE
HAALCRE	RACHAEL	Kit's aunt
UERDEPCN	PRUDENCE	Kit taught her to read and write
ITK	KIT	Came from Barbados
CYEMR	MERCY	Was crippled by a childhood illness
ONHJ	JOHN	Studying to be a minister
UIJDHT	JUDITH	Mercy's sister
IIMALWL	WILLIAM	Rich bachelor
TNA	NAT	Sailor
WTAETHM	MATTHEW	Kit's uncle
AHANHN	HANNAH	Quaker woman
LLEBKYUE	BULKELEY	The Reverend
RNASDO	ANDROS	Governor
LRBIBKCDA	BLACKBIRD	The Witch of ____ Pond
ESREPA	SPEARE	Author
OADBBSRA	BARBADOS	Kit's former home
OYSRKABO	SAYBROOK	Mistress Eaton spent her summers there
ABTO	BOAT	Kit jumped off the long ____ to get a doll
FCFUR	CRUFF	Goodwife ____; somber mother of Prudence
DWLEETIHFESR	WETHERSFIELD	Kit met John Holbrook on the boat to ____
THCWI	WITCH	Goodwife Cruff thought Kit was a ____ because she didn't drown
LYASP	PLAYS	Reading these for enjoyment was considered sinful
EHOLCTS	CLOTHES	Kit tried to give these to the Woods, but Matthew wouldn't allow it
UCHHRC	CHURCH	Kit detested going to ____ services
RTRTOIA	TRAITOR	Dr. Bulkeley thought Matthew was a ____
KQRUEA	QUAKER	Hannah Tupper's religion
LSROEFW	FLOWERS	Prudence left ____ for Kit
RBDI	BIRD	Nat compared Kit to a tropical ____
TLUNALMDEII	ILLUMINATED	A group of men ____ William's new home on Halloween
WEITR	WRITE	Kit taught Prudence to read and ____
PONHLID	DOLPHIN	Boat where Kit hid Hannah
ESMOU	MOUSE	The townspeople thought Hannah had changed herself into a ____
ESDH	SHED	Kit was locked in a ____ until her hearing

VOCABULARY RESOURCE MATERIALS

VOCABULARY WORD SEARCH - *The Witch of Blackbird Pond*

All words in this list are associated with *The Witch of Blackbird Pond* with an emphasis on the vocabulary words chosen for study in the text. The words are placed backwards, forward, diagonally, up and down. The included words are listed below.

```
T Z D B F K X D S R J G S L Y S L L Q Q B Z N M
G T S O S B S R S P B H T O R M U I H U J X F Z
M G R U W U B Y F R R S T Q B S N S Y H A B M R
P I L L O R Y L L U F E U R V E R I T A B L E P
X V N I L U I R S S X O M F X R R F D A P B M K
M X P F N L D E O A U F O O J W A E P N I T G S
R D O C I L E R S T F O R R S D I M D A I N E Y
F C E K V D P P A U C A I U P K R S E N P G E G
W U J T R E E O C C B I O T J E R Y T N U I R D
A D R M A R H L I L H R D Y I S R I R F D D S D
B N H T A U B E Y G O A M A T T M J E E U E E T
R L G T I K T M M M N E G G R I P R X S K L D J
L R I U V V P A I E H A D R D T U E A J G C L F
Z O D T I Z E T F P N L N A I S N N R I Y K O Y
N C J F H S M L S N Y T T T E N C O E R D K G M
J R L Y V E H A Y Z I E L I A T R V C G U H W K
J L B X P P L J C M D D N Y U C N Q T D N S R J
Q J X K K B R Y C F D O B A H I B H Q B C I C X
J Y L E T U L O S E R V R Y P X R P L M L F H Y
N O N C H A L A N C E Y L G N I Z I L A T N A T
```

AMENDED	DOCILE	MOCKERY	SANCTUARY
ANGUISH	DOWRIES	NONCHALANCE	SOBERED
ANNEXED	EXASPERATION	PAPIST	SURREPTITIOUSLY
ARDUOUS	FURTIVELY	PILLORY	SUSTAINED
BLASPHEMY	INEXORABLY	PIOUS	TANTALIZINGLY
BLITHELY	INFATUATED	POIGNANT	TIMOROUS
CHAGRIN	INFIDEL	QUALMS	VEHEMENTLY
CONTRADICTORY	INGENUITY	REFUGE	VERITABLE
CRONIES	INTIMIDATED	REPROOF	WISTFULLY
CUFF	INVEIGLED	RESOLUTELY	
DAFT	IRKSOME	RUEFULLY	

KEY: VOCABULARY WORD SEARCH - *The Witch of Blackbird Pond*

All words in this list are associated with *The Witch of Blackbird Pond* with an emphasis on the vocabulary words chosen for study in the text. The words are placed backwards, forward, diagonally, up and down. The included words are listed below.

```
            D                   S     S    Q
         S  O   S             O    U  I    U
            U W U   Y           B    N  S    A
   P I L L O R Y L L U F E U R V E R I T A B L E
         N I   U I R   S X O M   X   R F  A    M
         P F     D E O A U F O O   W A E P I       S
         D O C I L E R S T F O R R S D I M D A I N E
   F     E   V D P P A U C A I U P K   S E N P G E
         U   T   E E O C C B I O T   E R Y T N U I   D
   A     R   A R H L I L H R D Y I   R I R F D   S D
   B N   T A U   E Y G O A M A T T M   E E U E E T
      L G T I   T   M M N E G   R I P R X S K L D
         I U   V   A I E H A   R D T U E A   G C L
      O   T I   E T F P N   N A I S N N R I     O Y
   N       H S   L S N   T T E N C O E R         M
            E H A Y   I E L I A T   V C G U
            L       D   N Y U   N       N S
            B   Y       O   A I         I
      Y L E T U L O S E R   R
   N O N C H A L A N C E Y L G N I Z I L A T N A T
```

AMENDED	DOCILE	MOCKERY	SANCTUARY
ANGUISH	DOWRIES	NONCHALANCE	SOBERED
ANNEXED	EXASPERATION	PAPIST	SURREPTITIOUSLY
ARDUOUS	FURTIVELY	PILLORY	SUSTAINED
BLASPHEMY	INEXORABLY	PIOUS	TANTALIZINGLY
BLITHELY	INFATUATED	POIGNANT	TIMOROUS
CHAGRIN	INFIDEL	QUALMS	VEHEMENTLY
CONTRADICTORY	INGENUITY	REFUGE	VERITABLE
CRONIES	INTIMIDATED	REPROOF	WISTFULLY
CUFF	INVEIGLED	RESOLUTELY	
DAFT	IRKSOME	RUEFULLY	

VOCABULARY CROSSWORD - *The Witch of Blackbird Pond*

VOCABULARY CROSSWORD CLUES - *The Witch of Blackbird Pond*

ACROSS

1. A patronizing manner or behavior
6. Silly, foolish, insane, crazy
7. To strike with open hand; a slap or blow
9. Great suffering as from worry, grief or pain
12. To annoy by constant complaining or scolding
13. Atlantic or Pacific, for example
14. Longing pensively; expressing vague yearnings
18. State of being vexed, irritated, or annoyed
21. Sailor
22. Negative reply
23. Past tense of to sit
24. Tiresome; irritating; annoying
26. Kit jumped off the long ___ to get a doll
29. Made better; changed or revised
31. To bear through hardships; tolerate
32. Ingredient in ocean water
33. Nat compared Kit to a tropical ___
34. Has permission to
36. Contemptuous speech or action against God
38. Feeling or showing regret
39. Studying to be a minister
41. Belonging to you
45. Difficult to do
48. Showing a fixed, firm purpose; determined
50. Pronoun for belonging to Nat
51. Governor
52. That's all; there is no more; the ---
53. Opposite of on
54. Remain

DOWN

1. Mortification; embarrassment
2. Distress signal
3. Characterized by reason, sanity or self-control
4. Feelings of uneasiness or doubt
5. Very careful about every detail of behavior
6. The property a woman brings to her husband at marriage
8. Boats sail; airplanes ___
10. Gradually, slightly, so as to be difficult to perceive
11. Carried away by shallow love or affection
15. A place of refuge or protection
16. Done or acting in a stealthy way; sneaky
17. Came from Barbados
19. Added or attached
20. One who does not believe in a particular religion
25. Maintained
27. Unusual
28. Timid; full of or subject to fear
30. Easy to manage or discipline
35. Rebuke; censure; find fault with
37. Seemingly virtuous; showing religious devotion
40. The townspeople thought Hannah had changed herself into a ___
42. Goodwife ___; somber mother of Prudence
43. Reading these for enjoyment was considered sinful
44. Was crippled by a childhood illness
46. To be carried by a carriage or on horseback
47. Kit was locked in a ___ until her hearing
49. You row a boat with one

VOCABULARY CROSSWORD ANSWER KEY - *The Witch of Blackbird Pond*

VOCABULARY WORKSHEET 1 - *The Witch of Blackbird Pond*

____ 1. Gradually, slightly, so as to be difficult to perceive
    A. Anguish   B. Imperceptibly   C. Poignant   D. Wistfully

____ 2. Showing a fixed, firm purpose; determined
    A. Mockery   B. Pillory   C. Resolutely   D. Punctilious

____ 3. Rashly; impulsively; done suddenly with little thought
    A. Impetuously   B. Cronies   C. Anguish   D. Veritable

____ 4. Feeling or showing regret
    A. Inveigled   B. Resolutely   C. Ruefully   D. Amended

____ 5. Very careful about every detail of behavior
    A. Punctilious   B. Tantalizingly   C. Pious   D. Vehemently

____ 6. Seemingly virtuous; showing religious devotion
    A. Cuff   B. Papist   C. Pious   D. Anguish

____ 7. State of being vexed, irritated, or annoyed
    A. Vehemently   B. Exasperation   C. Pillory   D. Arduous

____ 8. Emotionally touching or moving; pungent smell or taste
    A. Papist   B. Furtively   C. Punctilious   D. Poignant

____ 9. Tiresome; irritating; annoying
    A. Tantalizingly   B. Irksome   C. Punctilious   D. Blithely

____ 10. A patronizing manner or behavior
    A. Condescension   B. Imperceptibly   C. Daft   D. Reproof

____ 11. One who does not believe in a particular religion
    A. Impetuously   B. Pillory   C. Qualms   D. Infidel

____ 12. Characterized by reason, sanity or self-control
    A. Sobered   B. Consternation   C. Annexed   D. Chagrin

____ 13. Mortification; embarrassment
    A. Chagrin   B. Arduous   C. Inexorably   D. Tantalizingly

____ 14. Led by deception; enticed or tricked into something
    A. Veritable   B. Sanctuary   C. Inveigled   D. Impetuously

____ 15. In a secret, stealthy way; clandestine
    A. Surreptitiously   B. Incredulous   C. Poignant   D. Tantalizingly

____ 16. In fact; actual; truly
    A. Punctilious   B. Veritable   C. Resolutely   D. Vehemently

____ 17. Added or attached
    A. Annexed   B. Exhilarating   C. Veritable   D. Ingenuity

____ 18. A place of safety
    A. Incredulous   B. Refuge   C. Mockery   D. Provocatively

____ 19. Made afraid; made timid; cowed
    A. Intimidated   B. Timorous   C. Cuff   D. Irksome

____ 20. Great fear or shock that makes one feel helpless
    A. Consternation   B. Blasphemy   C. Chagrin   D. Reproof

KEY: VOCABULARY WORKSHEET 1 - *The Witch of Blackbird Pond*

_B_ 1. Gradually, slightly, so as to be difficult to perceive
    A. Anguish   B. Imperceptibly   C. Poignant   D. Wistfully

_C_ 2. Showing a fixed, firm purpose; determined
    A. Mockery   B. Pillory   C. Resolutely   D. Punctilious

_A_ 3. Rashly; impulsively; done suddenly with little thought
    A. Impetuously   B. Cronies   C. Anguish   D. Veritable

_C_ 4. Feeling or showing regret
    A. Inveigled   B. Resolutely   C. Ruefully   D. Amended

_A_ 5. Very careful about every detail of behavior
    A. Punctilious   B. Tantalizingly   C. Pious   D. Vehemently

_C_ 6. Seemingly virtuous; showing religious devotion
    A. Cuff   B. Papist   C. Pious   D. Anguish

_B_ 7. State of being vexed, irritated, or annoyed
    A. Vehemently   B. Exasperation   C. Pillory   D. Arduous

_D_ 8. Emotionally touching or moving; pungent smell or taste
    A. Papist   B. Furtively   C. Punctilious   D. Poignant

_B_ 9. Tiresome; irritating; annoying
    A. Tantalizingly   B. Irksome   C. Punctilious   D. Blithely

_A_ 10. A patronizing manner or behavior
    A. Condescension   B. Imperceptibly   C. Daft   D. Reproof

_D_ 11. One who does not believe in a particular religion
    A. Impetuously   B. Pillory   C. Qualms   D. Infidel

_A_ 12. Characterized by reason, sanity or self-control
    A. Sobered   B. Consternation   C. Annexed   D. Chagrin

_A_ 13. Mortification; embarrassment
    A. Chagrin   B. Arduous   C. Inexorably   D. Tantalizingly

_C_ 14. Led by deception; enticed or tricked into something
    A. Veritable   B. Sanctuary   C. Inveigled   D. Impetuously

_A_ 15. In a secret, stealthy way; clandestine
    A. Surreptitiously   B. Incredulous   C. Poignant   D. Tantalizingly

_B_ 16. In fact; actual; truly
    A. Punctilious   B. Veritable   C. Resolutely   D. Vehemently

_A_ 17. Added or attached
    A. Annexed   B. Exhilarating   C. Veritable   D. Ingenuity

_B_ 18. A place of safety
    A. Incredulous   B. Refuge   C. Mockery   D. Provocatively

_A_ 19. Made afraid; made timid; cowed
    A. Intimidated   B. Timorous   C. CUFF   D. Irksome

_A_ 20. Great fear or shock that makes one feel helpless
    A. Consternation   B. Blasphemy   C. Chagrin   D. Reproof

VOCABULARY WORKSHEET 2 - *The Witch of Blackbird Pond*

____ 1. REFUGE   A. Easy to manage or discipline

____ 2. CUFF   B. Characterized by reason, sanity or self-control

____ 3. SANCTUARY   C. Added or attached

____ 4. PROVOCATIVELY D. Great fear or shock that makes one feel helpless

____ 5. INFIDEL   E. Old friends; close companions

____ 6. EXHILARATING F. Difficult to do

____ 7. SOBERED   G. Invigorating or stimulating

____ 8. ARDUOUS   H. Tending to provoke as to action, thought or feeling

____ 9. DOCILE   I. The property a woman brings to her husband at marriage

____ 10. UNPREMEDITATED   J. Done or acting in a stealthy way; sneaky

____ 11. CRONIES   K. Impassioned; fervently

____ 12. VEHEMENTLY   L. One who does not believe in a particular religion

____ 13. FURTIVELY   M. A place of refuge or protection

____ 14. QUALMS   N. To strike with open hand; a slap or blow

____ 15. MOCKERY   O. A place of safety

____ 16. BLITHELY   P. Ridicule; false, derisive or impertinent imitation

____ 17. ANNEXED   Q. Showing a gay, cheerful disposition; carefree

____ 18. CONTRADICTORY R. Feelings of uneasiness or doubt

____ 19. CONSTERNATION S. Done without any plan or forethought

____ 20. DOWRIES   T. Asserting the opposite of what someone else said

KEY: VOCABULARY WORKSHEET 2 - *The Witch of Blackbird Pond*

_O_	1. REFUGE	A.	Easy to manage or discipline
_N_	2. CUFF	B.	Characterized by reason, sanity or self-control
_M_	3. SANCTUARY	C.	Added or attached
_H_	4. PROVOCATIVELY	D.	Great fear or shock that makes one feel helpless
_L_	5. INFIDEL	E.	Old friends; close companions
_G_	6. EXHILARATING	F.	Difficult to do
_B_	7. SOBERED	G.	Invigorating or stimulating
_F_	8. ARDUOUS	H.	Tending to provoke as to action, thought or feeling
_A_	9. DOCILE	I.	The property a woman brings to her husband at marriage
_S_	10. UNPREMEDITATED	J.	Done or acting in a stealthy way; sneaky
_E_	11. CRONIES	K.	Impassioned; fervently
_K_	12. VEHEMENTLY	L.	One who does not believe in a particular religion
_J_	13. FURTIVELY	M.	A place of refuge or protection
_R_	14. QUALMS	N.	To strike with open hand; a slap or blow
_P_	15. MOCKERY	O.	A place of safety
_Q_	16. BLITHELY	P.	Ridicule; false, derisive or impertinent imitation
_C_	17. ANNEXED	Q.	Showing a gay, cheerful disposition; carefree
_T_	18. CONTRADICTORY	R.	Feelings of uneasiness or doubt
_D_	19. CONSTERNATION	S.	Done without any plan or forethought
_I_	20. DOWRIES	T.	Asserting the opposite of what someone else said

VOCABULARY JUGGLE LETTER REVIEW GAME CLUES - *The Witch of Blackbird Pond*

SCRAMBLED	WORD	CLUE
YWLIFTUSL	WISTFULLY	Longing pensively; expressing vague yearnings
UNSAGHI	ANGUISH	Great suffering as from worry, grief or pain
UFCF	CUFF	To strike with open hand; a slap or blow
ADTF	DAFT	Silly, foolish, insane, crazy
AENCONNACLH	NONCHALANCE	Showing cool lack of concern
FYULRETVI	FURTIVELY	Done or acting in a stealthy way; sneaky
SPUUONICLTI	PUNCTILIOUS	Very careful about every detail of behavior
YRILPCMTBEPIE	IMPERCEPTIBLY	Gradually, slightly, so as to be difficult to perceive
OFORPER	REPROOF	Rebuke; censure; find fault with
XNITAAGELHIR	EXHILARATING	Invigorating or stimulating
NEIATTDIMID	INTIMIDATED	Made afraid; made timid; cowed
HGNIRCA	CHAGRIN	Mortification; embarrassment
EPRSAATXINOE	EXASPERATION	State of being vexed, irritated, or annoyed
MOSKRIE	IRKSOME	Tiresome; irritating; annoying
CCDSEEINNNOOS	CONDESCENSION	A patronizing manner or behavior
RLIEYXNAOB	INEXORABLY	Unrelentingly; cannot be stopped
MURTOSOI	TIMOROUS	Timid; full of or subject to fear
EVELRABTI	VERITABLE	In fact; actual; truly
SOUPI	PIOUS	Seemingly virtuous; showing religious devotion
GREFEU	REFUGE	A place of safety
RYLEUETOSL	RESOLUTELY	Showing a fixed, firm purpose; determined
MALUQS	QUALMS	Feelings of uneasiness or doubt
RCYKOEM	MOCKERY	Ridicule; false, derisive or impertinent imitation
TATNDAFEUI	INFATUATED	Carried away by shallow love or affection
OVOCRVPYALETI	PROVOCATIVELY	Tending to provoke as to action, thought or feeling
UYPILMUTOSE	IMPETUOUSLY	Rashly; impulsively; done suddenly with little thought
DSIEUNUCLRO	INCREDULOUS	Doubting; skeptical; unwilling or unable to believe
TUCYSRANA	SANCTUARY	A place of refuge or protection

Witch of Blackbird Pond Vocabulary Juggle Letter Review Game Clues Continued

XEEDNAN	ANNEXED	Added or attached
TPSAIP	PAPIST	A Roman Catholic; one who believes in papal supremacy
YMLBEHSAP	BLASPHEMY	Contemptuous speech or action against God
OLRLYIP	PILLORY	A wooden device into which petty offenders were locked and exposed to public ridicule
UFYLURLE	RUEFULLY	Feeling or showing regret
HBYETILL	BLITHELY	Showing a gay, cheerful disposition; carefree
TNIGNYIUE	INGENUITY	Cleverness, originality, skill
GOATPINN	POIGNANT	Emotionally touching or moving; pungent smell or taste
TANTOERSNICON	CONSTERNATION	Great fear or shock that makes one feel helpless
LEDFINI	INFIDEL	One who does not believe in a particular religion
AAZYTNIGLNLIT	TANTALIZINGLY	Teasingly
ODELIC	DOCILE	Easy to manage or discipline
BREDSEO	SOBERED	Characterized by reason, sanity or self-control
ISTUDNESA	SUSTAINED	Maintained
GNIDLVIEE	INVEIGLED	Led by deception; enticed or tricked into something
RSEOCIN	CRONIES	Old friends; close companions
YMELVHTENE	VEHEMENTLY	Impassioned; fervently
TLRPIISTYURUOES	SURREPTITIOUSLY	In a secret, stealthy way; clandestine
CYORNOTTRCAID	CONTRADICTORY	Asserting the opposite of what someone else said
UDSUARO	ARDUOUS	Difficult to do
NEDMEAD	AMENDED	Made better; changed or revised
RIWEOSD	DOWRIES	The property a woman brings to her husband at marriage
EDMIETRAPTNEUD	UNPREMEDITATED	Done without any plan or forethought

www.ingramcontent.com/pod-product-compliance
Lightning Source LLC
Chambersburg PA
CBHW051413070526

44584CB00023B/3408